TELL
YOUR
STORY
to the
WORLD
& *SELL IT FOR*
MILLIONS

KENNETH ATCHITY *and* LISA CERASOLI
with CHELSEA MONGIRD

STORY MERCHANT BOOKS

LOS ANGELES • 2018

Tell Your Story to the World & Sell It for Millions

www.kenatchity.blogspot.com

ISBN-13: 978-1-7323411-1-1

Story Merchant Books
400 S. Burnside Ave. #11B
Los Angeles, CA 90036
www.storymerchantbooks.com

Interior Design: Lauren Michelle, www.529books.com
Cover Design: Claire Moore, www.529books.com

At last—someone wrote the book every screenwriter has needed for years. It can make the difference between success and failure in the industry.

—Linda Seger, author *Making a Good Script Great*

Sell Your Story to Hollywood:

I've never read a book that more concisely and accurately tells writers how to sell to Hollywood in today's market. Stop whatever it is you're doing and read it. Ken Atchity, a master storyteller himself, knows this world.

—Michael A. Simpson, President, Informant Media Entertainment

If you ever wished for a map to your dreams as a screenwriter, Ken's book pretty much has the process satellite scanned in.

—Pen Densham, Oscar-nominated filmmaker/producer/writer of 15 features, including *Robin Hood Prince of Thieves*

MUST READ. Kenneth Atchity's book is the golden machete-of-knowledge writers need to survive in the entertainment industry's unruly jungle.

—Todd Klick, writer/producer, author of *Beat by Beat*

No one I know covers the spectrum of storytelling more thoroughly than my friend, Ken Atchity. As a scholar, educator, author, publisher, and film producer, Ken has been an integral part of every aspect of film producing from the inside and out. As a former Hollywood agent, studio creative executive, and independent producer of dozens of films, I recommend that anyone with dreams and aspirations to be part of the creative process that realizes a completed and marketed film or television program heed the absolutely accurate advice of *Sell Your Story to Hollywood*.

—Norman Stephens, Emmy and Peabody Award-winning producer, former exec at Warner Television & Village Roadshow Pictures

How to Quit Your Day Job and Live Out Your Dreams:

A valuable guide in sorting out your choice of a right livelihood.
Everyone should read it.
> —James Butler, vice president of the Council for Aid to Education

Having successfully gone through the type of career transition
described in this book, I can appreciate not only its masterful detailing
of the process but also its thoughtful, thought-provoking challenge to
those thinking of undergoing their own transitions.
> —Ira Wohl, Academy Award-winning director

This book addresses "who you are" as the starting point for "what you
do." The more you know yourself, the more confidence you will have
about doing work that fits you. And the more you know about
yourself, the more you will recognize the freedom you have in
choosing work that is meaningful, purposeful, and profitable. It
doesn't matter if you are eighteen or sixty-eight; this process can work
for you.
> —Dan Miller, author of *48 Days to the Work You Love*

Atchity tells you how to be a 'Type C,' how to choose only the kind of
stress that brings pleasure, how to squeeze every ounce of creativity
out of your being, how to live life to the fullest.
> —Howard Owen, author of *Littlejohn* and *Fat Lightning*

Homer's Iliad: The Shield of Memory:

I know of no better introduction to this splendid poem. In fact, I
know of no other book as good.
> —John Gardner, professor, editor, author of
> *The Sunlight Dialogues* and *Grendel*

PRAISE FOR OTHER WORKS BY LISA CERASOLI:

As Nora Jo Fades Away

"Unruly entertaining, glaringly heartbreaking…. I dare you to put this book down."
>—Cory Schuelke, Partner & CFO, Revelry Music Group; Financial Consultant, Lionsgate Music & Publishing

"Upon beginning the book, I quickly realized meals could wait. This is a true, inspirational story. One that must be read by anyone dealing with Alzheimer's…or simply anyone."
>—Lee Adams, Retired English Professor, East Central College

"The first thing that strikes you about Cerasoli's memoir is her steadfast refusal to manipulate us. Instead of tugging at our heartstrings to produce easy tears, she writes with a rigorous, clear-eyed lack of sentimentality and sly humor, which only heightens the book's emotional impact. Nora Jo… is a passionate tribute to an unforgettable woman and a lesson in love under seemingly impossible circumstances."
>—Rob Potter, Story Analyst, HBO and Castle Rock Entertainment

"As seen in her previous work, *As Nora Jo Fades Away* once again showcases Lisa Cerasoli's brilliant ability to weave wit and warmth into grim subject matter. This memoir is a refreshing reflection of an inevitable human consideration: What would you do if faced with the responsibility of an aging loved one?"
>—Bill Hinkle, Television Producer, CNN

14 Days with Alzheimer's

"One of those exceptional films where you find yourself either laughing or crying, often within seconds. And, as heartbreaking as Alzheimer's is, the film also leaves you with a sense of peace."
>—*CityPulse* Magazine

Lucky Number 9: Journey of a Rubber Tapper's Daughter
by Rina Tham with Lisa Cerasoli

"Compelling! I think of the saying, "Courage is fear that has said its prayers." Tham's spiritual evolution was one of the most interesting parts of the story. I loved the descriptions of the jungle in Malaysia and the reunion with her father as a young adult is inspiring. I'd recommend this book to anyone who wants to motivate young people to dream big dreams and work hard to achieve them. Tham is well served by her co-writer Lisa Cerasoli. Great job, gals!"

—Maggie Gwinn, MFT, Jungian Analyst

"Emotional, at times heartbreaking, colorful, optimistic, adventurous, strong, and encouraging, this book will hardly leave anyone indifferent. Expect punches, and even knock downs for a few minutes as you are reading it."

—Five Star Review

"This book teaches you how to be fearless and live with an open heart. It's a perfect example of how to be adventurous and embrace life with open arms. You won't be able to put it down until you're finished reading it—a must-read for everyone."

—Five Star Review

Through Fire and Rain: Surviving the Impossible with Love, Music, and Modern Medicine
by MaryAnn and Joseph Anselmo with Lisa Cerasoli

"One of the most inspirational books I've ever read. A truly amazing story of love, faith, and the art of never giving up. MaryAnn Anselmo is a hero in every way. Joseph Anselmo is a man who sets an example of love and devotion for everyone to learn from. When I wake up tomorrow I'll see the world differently. My heart just got a reset. 'Let's make something of every day we have.'"

—Gennaro S. Tedesco

"A beautiful and touching story about never underestimating the power of love, perseverance, and determination. I read this entire book in one sitting. This story has touched my heart, and I am looking forward to the sequel! Well done!"

—Lisa Williams

"The Anselmos demonstrate a resourceful and innovative attitude in dealing with true life-threatening issues. You will be inspired to not allow circumstances to dictate your outlook on life. Additionally, the book includes numerous resources for those wishing to research questions about similar health problems. Just read it."

—Five Star Review

On the Brink of Bliss and Insanity

"The characters are smashing, and the story is outrageous, and touching. As wild as *My Best Friend's Wedding*, as hilarious as *There's Something About Mary*."

—Geri Aheam, Reviewer and Top Contributor

"From the first page, I thought, I'm going to read this book again…soon. I hope to see more from this author in the near future!"

—Five Star Review

"Most of us crack open a new novel for the same reason. We want to be transfixed, tantalized, or simply transported to another space entirely. *On the Brink…* gives this to you in spades. Cerasoli will knock you sideways with her unabashed humor. No stone of inner turmoil is left unturned in her painting of "Annie" or her sculpture of "Billy." All of Cerasoli's characters vibrate and come alive in this wry and witty account of what could really be each and every one us while we floundered around in our twenties."

—Mile High Reader

This book is a basic beginner's guide for amateur storytellers who have no idea how to become professional storytellers. Others are profiting from their storytelling. Why not you?

ACKNOWLEDGMENTS

This book evolved for at least a decade and, in whole or in part, passed before so many critical eyes we wouldn't know where to begin thanking our clients and professional readers, partners, and industry allies from whom we learned everything incorporated here. But standouts include AEI President Chi-Li Wong, television producing partner Norman Stephens, webinar partner Daniel Hall, Laurence O'Brian, and Story Merchant interns Lucas Moore, Derrick Iloenyosi, and Anson Petrick. We appreciate Claire Moore's persistence on the cover design, and we thank editors Danielle Canfield, Adrian Muraro, and Lauren Michelle for their diligence and attention to detail.

CONTENTS

TELL
YOUR
STORY
to the
WORLD
& SELL IT FOR
MILLIONS

"My friends, we have a chance to become Big Publishing's worst nightmare."

—Stephen King
The Plant
(…on becoming the first major author to direct-publish an e-book
in installments in the spring of 2000)

In 2010, **Amanda Hocking** was sitting penniless in a tiny, Ikea-furnished apartment in Austin, Minnesota. She had heard about an upcoming Muppets exhibit in Chicago that summer. She loved the Muppets! But it would take $300 to get there, so she uploaded one of her many turned-down **novels** as an e-book. Six months later, 150,000 copies were sold, more than enough to cover the trip. Within twenty months, she sold 1.5 million e-books, making $2.5 million.

Amanda Hocking had been fed up with attempts to find a **traditional publisher** [words that appear in **bold face** are defined in "Story Market Terms" at the end] for her **Young Adult** paranormal novels. She **direct-published** and began selling her novels at online bookstores like Amazon and Barnesandnoble.com. Most were low-priced (99¢ to $2.99) digital downloads. Hocking credits her success to aggressive self-promotion through her blog, Facebook, Twitter, and word of mouth, as well as writing in a popular **genre**—her books star trolls, vampires, and zombies (*My Blood Approves* and *The Hollows* series). She also discovered **book bloggers**. "I asked them if they'd be interested in reviewing my books, and most of them said yes, even if they didn't generally review self-published work."

That's how she did it; that was the secret to her success.

Amanda Hocking blazed her way to success with direct publishing. We've entered a new frontier where if writers can't get signed by an **agent** and published traditionally, they no longer have to play the waiting game.

PART I

I believe in the power of stories to change the world. We'll interrupt anything—work, dinner, exercise, meditation, sex—to take in a dramatic story: the latest terrorist attack, the latest political scandal, the latest miraculous brush with death. Swapping stories reassures us, binds us together as human beings, makes us comfortable with our crazy world by giving us a feeling of being in control. Stories educate, make us laugh, win elections, give us courage, entertain. Stories save lives. Every human transaction begins, and sometimes ends, with, "What's your story?"

—Kenneth Atchity, Story Merchant

1

THE POWER OF STORYTELLING

A CAJUN IS WALKING BACK up to his pickup from the bayou when he comes upon a game warden.

"What's that you got there on that stringer?" the game warden asks.

"Half a dozen pan-sized sac-a-lait," the Cajun answers.

"Do you know they're out of season right now?" the game warden asks, reaching for his citation pad.

That takes the Cajun by surprise. "But these are my pet fishes," he finally says.

"Your *pet* fishes! Now I've heard everything. Where are you going with them if they're your pet fish?"

"I'm taking them back home. Every Saturday morning, I bring them down to the bayou and let them swim around a little. Then I clap my hands and they come back so we can go home."

"You in trouble, boy," the game warden says. "You think I was born yesterday? I'd have to see that with my own eyes or you in a mess of trouble."

They walk down to the bayou together, and the Cajun lets the fish go. Sure enough, they swim happily away.

After a few minutes, the game warden says, "Well…go ahead."

"Go ahead and what?" the Cajun says.

"Clap your hands and call them back!"

"Call who back?" the Cajun asks.

Whether it's a hearty laugh or a deep feeling of hopefulness, from the bayou banks to the oceanside, from the country front porch, the cozy winter hearth, the hunters' campfire, the chambers of the Supreme Court, stories change lives.

"What's your story?" is the question behind each human encounter with a stranger because, indeed, we judge a person by his story. Whether it's girl meets boy, speeder meets traffic judge, evangelist begging his congregation for forgiveness, astronaut meets alien, or politician double-talking his way out of a tight spot, we learn about **character**, and how to cope with life's ups and downs—from stories.

We also define ourselves to others through storytelling. "I'm the person that jumps in and out of relationships," is *not* the kind of story you'd be telling your blind date, especially if your blind date turns out to be a "keeper"—although you might tell that story at a speed-dating event if you're across the table from someone whose eyes keep darting around the room, looking everywhere but at you.

We learn more from stories than we do from almost any other form of communication. Simply put, a good story is hard to forget, just as a bad story—one that has no clear point, one that is hopelessly complicated, one that feels irrelevant to the listener—is forgotten immediately. If the response is negative, you explain, "I just didn't like his story. I just didn't buy it."

2

Our stories define us as individuals. Their literary and **cinematic** equivalents shape our culture. Moviegoing is an active communication between audience and film. We receive the message, we internalize it, we process it, and we use it in our own stories and behavior.

Storytelling is the mind and heart's counterpart to sex—an essential act of communication by which the vital essence of our lives is exchanged and life itself is perpetuated. The person who tells a story evokes another from his audience; you read a good book, you want to share it with a friend.

Maybe your knack for storytelling started, as mine did, growing up listening to and spinning yarns on a rustic front porch for cousins willing to bring me out soft drinks, coffee, blackberry wine, or arrowheads in return for holding their attention. I reached the conclusion that there may be more to storytelling than self-gratification when I saw tears in their eyes or got them breaking into fits of laughter. This learning curve was further sharpened by the negative examples of my dear late departed Uncle Ed. He'd be on the other side of the porch, trapping one hapless cousin after another with the endless tale of how he peeled an orange in a war zone. Because poor Uncle Ed was unable to distinguish between too much detail and the big dramatic **twists** and turns needed to keep a story moving forward, my cousins appeared to be in physical pain when Uncle Ed spun a tale.

Uncle Wilbur, on the other hand, instinctually knew what Uncle Ed didn't—how to play on the hunger of his audience, how to use it as an invisible magician's wire that connected his storyteller's soul with theirs. I noticed that this happened even if—especially if—he was telling a story he'd told a dozen times before.

Uncle Wib was my first mentor.

3

"Not that one again!" he'd protest when they'd ask him to tell them the Pet Fish joke.

"Yes, we love that one!" they'd reply. "And Rosemary here hasn't heard it."

So, he'd tell it again, this time a little differently—out of respect to most of his audience who'd heard it so many times before.

Like many of you, I was a natural-born storyteller, but I was in South Louisiana (not quite NYC or LA). My audience, while mesmerized, was mainly blood relatives. My earnings for a story well told consisted mainly of arrowheads and blackberries. And they were great, but I couldn't imagine anyone paying me *money* to tell stories.

Maybe your storytelling career started as Lisa's did. She grew up in small-town America, too, in the Upper Peninsula of Michigan—God's Country.

She came out of the womb a talker. At home, this proved to be great fun. But at school, though she got mainly As, they went along with a string of detentions thanks to her 'round-the-clock storytelling propensity. She then discovered the theater, and thought, *this is where I can be a vehicle to tell stories to the world.* Lisa experienced deep satisfaction from acting, but it wasn't enough for the storyteller in her. In her mid-twenties, while under contract on a TV series, she wrote her first **feature film**, a romantic **comedy**.

That's where I came in. Lisa's script read very much like a novel—it was a character-driven **ensemble piece**. I dared her to start writing novels. This was the nudge she needed.

Now, fifteen-plus years later, we're giving you the nudge you need to tell your story to the world.

One day in town, at Walmart, you spot a headline: *First-time Novelist Sells Story to Hollywood for Six Million Dollars!* You read on. Another writer, a "screenwriter," is going to adapt it for the screen for three million dollars.

Your blood races. Why couldn't that be you?

Maybe your stories, too, are worth more than blackberry wine, Choctaw arrowheads, and detentions.

If you're like most people, you have a story to tell. *60 Minutes* once reported that one out of three people listed in the phonebook believe they have a story in them. They just don't know what to do about it.

This book lays out the world of the professional storyteller, where authors like J. K. Rowling (Harry Potter series—more than 400 million books sold) and James Patterson (fifty-six novels on the *New York Times* Bestseller List, eleven of them hitting #1) count annual earnings in not six or seven but eight figures. It's a world in which, literally, you can tell your story to the world and make millions. According to *Entertainment Weekly,* twenty-seven of Nora Roberts' books are sold every minute.

Today's worldwide story market is insatiable. What other industry could lure Janet Evanovich away from her longtime publisher Random House for a forty-million, three-book deal? Where else could dozens of screenwriters be paid over two million dollars for **studio** scripts?

After nearly twenty years of teaching comparative literature and creative writing to undergraduates at Occidental College, and to adult students at UCLA's Writers Program and the Learning Annex, I moved from the academic world of literary criticism—analyzing, reviewing, and judging stories—to the professional story marketplace as a writer, **producer**, and **literary manager**. I started finding, creating, developing, perfecting, and *selling* stories to publishers and production companies. A visiting ambassador gave me the epithet "story merchant," and pointed out that I was following in the wake of my Phoenician ancestors, who brought the alphabet of stories from ancient port to ancient port. I quickly learned that no one places a higher value on stories than New York publishing and Hollywood entertainment. The next bestselling novel or headline story is so sought after that a whole profession has sprung up around seeking it. These "**trackers**" do nothing but track down unpublished stories and report them to their employers—publishing companies and film studios.

I learned that breaking in was extremely difficult for writers on both coasts. Coming off a full career already, and therefore older than others breaking in, I decided to learn the business side of show business to help my writer clients achieve their dreams sooner rather than later. After years of apprenticeship—reading contracts, meeting with editors and executives, hearing writers' war stories of both failure and success—I started getting the knack for the story marketplace and figured out how to get my clients' novels published and then turn them into movies that got produced.

I love discovering a book like James Michael Pratt's direct-published but barely edited *The Last Valentine*. My company, Writer's Lifeline, gave the book the editing it deserved, and then my management company sold it to a major New York publisher, who pushed it to *New York Times* bestseller status. Then our production company set it up in Hollywood and saw it

become, after some years in **development**, a CBS film starring Betty White and Jennifer Love Hewitt (*The Lost Valentine*, Hallmark Hall of Fame's highest-rated film in years). Curious about "Last" vs. "Lost"? The

President of Hallmark Cards told me at lunch at Kansas City's Alameda Plaza, "You'll never see *this* company make a movie called *The* Last *Valentine!*" (Following the movie debut, the reissue of James's bestseller by St. Martin's Press was also called *The Lost Valentine.*)

Another effective **scenario** for us is taking a script and working with a storyteller (novelist) to develop an already-written screenplay into a novel. My companies did this with Royce Buckingham's *Demon Keeper.* We then sold both the novel to a publisher (Putnam) and the screenplay to a studio (Fox 2000).

In our encounters with other managers, producers, studio execs, attorneys, coaches, and agents, we found ourselves agreeing with them about one thing: it is *never* a great plan to submit a terrific concept that is unprofessionally executed. Because **gatekeepers** in the story market are inundated with stories that fall under the definition of best and second-best, they don't have time for that "third-best" project. They aren't wasting away in Amateurville.

But, like other gatekeepers, we kept running into good ideas presented weakly—so many that, in 1996, I founded an editorial development company (www.thewriterslifeline.com) and Lisa founded www.529books.com in 2013. Both companies serve storytellers wishing to move to the next stage in their writer's growth, "bringing their craft and technique to the level of their talent and ambition." Our companies became sort of farm teams, shaping writers up for the big leagues. One of Writer's Lifeline's early success stories was a **manuscript** titled *White Scream,* submitted by a kosher meatpacker in South Florida with a mighty vision, Steve Alten. The book had been turned down by fifty agents and publishers. After re-

7

development with The Writer's Lifeline, the manuscript was refined into *Meg*, and my then-management and production company, Atchity Entertainment International, concluded a multi-million-dollar sale to Doubleday-Bantam and then Disney (the movie, retitled *The Meg*, appeared from Warner Bros, directed by Jon Turtletaub and starring Jason Statham, in 2018). Steve Alten went on to publish a dozen more novels.

John Scott Shepherd's *Henry's List of Wrongs*, another Writer's Lifeline novel, sold at auction to New Line Pictures for $1.2 million. It was published by Rugged Land/Pocket Books as Shepherd's first novel and the foundation of a multimillion-dollar film and television career that also produced *Joe Somebody* and *Life or Something Like It*, as well as TV series *You Me Her, Save Me,* and *See Kate Run*. After a lifetime of experience as a writer, teacher, motivator, producer, manager, and career coach for all kinds of successful writers, I still wake up excited about the next great story.

Because it is based primarily on hands-on experience, the advice in this book is more *descriptive* than *prescriptive*. This means you should feel free to follow your own common sense and instinct to adapt, alter, or transform what you read here to suit yourself, your story, and your circumstances. We want to help you by *describing* how amateur writers have achieved commercial success, and by outlining the skills you'll need to get started and feel confident.

Armed with the information we've gathered in *Tell Your Story to the World & Sell It for Millions*—and your persistence—you'll be set to succeed. You'll have separated yourself from all those storytellers who haven't done their homework and learned the ropes. You wouldn't *think* of selling real estate or practicing law without making whatever investment it takes to educate yourself and acquire the appropriate professional license. Yet amateur storytellers send their work to film companies and publishers, websites and music companies, without knowing the first thing about what to send, who to send it to, and how to send it. After reading this book along with our suggested readings, you'll separate yourself from them and succeed because you'll know what to do. You'll succeed because the thirst for well-told stories is universal and eternal. Because delivery systems will continue changing at an ever-accelerating pace. And, because the need for stories grows stronger as these communication channels proliferate. Stories magically lift the curtain on happier or more terrible times and events, giving us the opportunity to test our emotional responses in a safe environment—that of vicarious experience.

And if you remember to take your storytelling, but not yourself, too seriously, you'll learn the discipline required to make you the well-paid writer you deserve to be.

Your goal is to *be the best storyteller you can be.* The result will be your audience's positive response to your stories, which means that the storytelling industries will compensate you financially, and the reviewers (like I used to be for the *Los Angeles Times* Book Review) may even compensate you with appreciation—though reviews are generally best taken with a grain of salt by creators.

Personal gratification becomes a happy side effect of leading the life of a professional storyteller. Your most-fulfilling satisfaction is in telling the best story you can, and in improving your craft every day.

"How do you know a novel is great?" *Los Angeles Times* book editor Art Seidenbaum asked me at a panel one evening at the University of Judaism in Beverly Hills.

"A great novel changes your life," I responded. "And you'll know that because at first, you're so excited you can't read it fast enough. Then a point comes when you realize that the faster you read it, the sooner it will be over and, instead, you start reading it as slowly as you can, because you know you can only read it for the first time once."

––––––––––––––––––––––

Writing a book that causes that effect is the bar, the end-all, dope, the cat's ass.

The first question to ask yourself about an unwritten story that's keeping you up at night is this: *Is this indeed a great story that merits being turned into a great novel?*

If the answer is "no" or "maybe," save yourself the agony.

But if you answered "yes," keep reading!

We're writing this book to improve your life—and maybe the world—by urging you to tell the story you've been keeping inside till now, and showing you how to tell it and sell it. If you don't share your story, the world will never have it. If you have a story inside you, it's your responsibility to tell it. If you don't tell us your story, who will? Being a visionary is a vocation and a **mission**.

But how do you get from the porch to the podium? You've got the vision, and an inexhaustible supply of stories—some true, some made up, most in between. You've even got the talent. You can see that in the faces of your audiences. And you've gone so far as to pick up that successful writer's book—and that's when you realize, you don't really know how to write a story:

You've heard the phrase, "Start the book on page one," but you don't know how to do that.

How many words are in a book, anyway?

How many characters?

How many **chapters***?*

If these and other questions plague you, you are in what we've identified as "Stage 1" of a writer's growth. You have the storyteller's instincts but haven't yet learned the skills and techniques necessary to become a highly compensated, commercially successful novelist or screenwriter—one who could get a million dollars for your next book or script.

What's required next is self-education, "getting up to speed" on the profession you'd like to master. In today's world, there are three ways to do that:

1. The school of hard knocks, a.k.a. "the learning curve." You go at it on your own. Twenty years and hundreds of **rejection** slips later, you finally get it all together and, with some luck, break through.

2. You go to school for a creative writing degree, spending at least two years, or maybe more. You come out feeling educated…and broke. But you know how things work, and you're ready to go at it despite knowing the difficulties.

3. You read books like this one (only when you think you need them) and shave your learning curve in half.

That's our mission as your coaches: to shave years off your learning curve.

"Many people believed that if the writing was good, the author would be offered a traditional publishing deal."

After being rejected by a dozen agents, **Rachel Abbott** had no plans for direct publishing. Friends and family coaxed her into it, stating her book was great. In 2011, she published *Only the Innocent* on Amazon Kindle UK, and it shot to #1 in sales. By 2012, the book was the second bestselling direct-published title. She now has six books published and has sold over two million copies.

2

WHAT IS A STORY?

Leaping from Stage 1 to Stage 2 in Your Writer's Growth

STORIES ARE SLICES OF LIFE. They range in size from a five-second joke to a 140-character tweet; from Marcel Proust's *Remembrance of Things Past* (1,267,069 words) to Truman Capote's *Breakfast at Tiffany's* (26,433 words) or the bestselling memoir of all time, *Tuesdays with Morrie* (35,000 words); from J. R. R. Tolkien's *The Lord of the Rings* (488,103 words) to the Bible (nearly 800,000 words) and the Koran (143,840 words).

From Miguel de Cervantes, who wrote *Don Quixote* (often dubbed the first modern novel), to William Goldman (*Butch Cassidy and the Sundance Kid, The Princess Bride*), and Nobel and Pulitzer Prize-winning author Toni Morrison (*The Bluest Eye, Beloved*), a story is a communication mechanism told using characters' **action** and **dialogue** in a **narrative** of words and/or **images** to construct a fictional reality that entertains, instructs, or inspires audiences. By this definition, a Simpsons' comic strip is as much a story as *Anna Karenina*; a painting like Grant Wood's *American Gothic* is as much a story as the film *Deadpool*; a *New Yorker* cartoon or a thirty-second MasterCard "Priceless" commercial is as much a "story" as Elton

John's "Candle in the Wind" or Robert Frost's "The Road Not Taken."

Story is not life, but the refashioning of lifelike materials to provoke an intense response. The classical Greek philosopher Aristotle called doing that **mimesis, or imitation.** Stories look like life but display more vivid, immediate, and distinguishable patterns than life does. That is why we admire a great storyteller. He can take a life event that struck even the participant as mundane and turn it into a laugh, a warning, or a point he wants to illustrate. A man everyone in town knows as nasty makes a big show of being baptized in front of the whole population. On the ride home, the local storyteller sums it up: "That man is so mean that when they dunked him in the river, all the fish died."

Reality, for many people, offers too much **originality**—too much unpredictability—which is why we have a hard time trusting it, and why most people prefer stories to news.

Every story is fashioned from a collection of elements and ingredients that converge to create a single finished product. This finished product—the story—serves a purpose. It's a lesson (a moral, a warning), a message of empowerment (don't give up), a how-to (pursue your dreams, find love, travel the world on a dime, build an empire, get along with your spouse), or entertainment (through laughter or shock value).

Let's look closer at the five primary ingredients of a dramatic story:

1. It has strong characters:
   a. A well-defined, relatable (**"sympathetic"**) **protagonist**—from the Greek word "first actor," the one whose story it is. Around the protagonist, the storyteller builds the action.

15

b. A worthy **antagonist**—from the Greek "opponent." The antagonist acts against the protagonist; their **conflict** is the **drama** that moves the story forward.

2. A story has conflict, preferably in every **scene.**

3. It is made up of scenes, which are the units of drama.

4. The scenes have an overall **structure**—a **beginning**, a **middle**, and an **end**.

5. The story has a **theme**, a point—whether it's a laugh at the end of a joke, a moral lesson, or a terrifying fright.

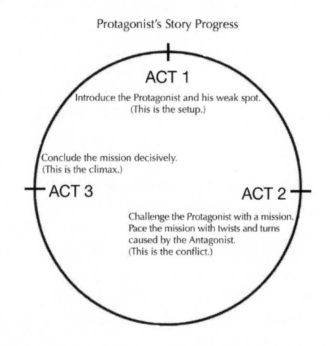

Protagonist's Story Progress

ACT 1
Introduce the Protagonist and his weak spot.
(This is the setup.)

Conclude the mission decisively.
(This is the climax.)
ACT 3

ACT 2
Challenge the Protagonist with a mission.
Pace the mission with twists and turns
caused by the Antagonist.
(This is the conflict.)

It should be a relief to realize that you could list *all* the necessary ingredients of a story on a single 3x5 card. Unlike the messiness of life, a story is a relatively simple construction that represents (or "imitates") life.

A good storyteller can tell a short version of a story:

"It's very hard to live in a studio apartment in San Jose with a man who's learning to play the violin." That's what she told the police when she handed them the empty revolver. (Richard Brautigan "The Scarlatti Tilt," from *Revenge of the Lawn*)

Or he can tell a long version, like Pat Conroy's *The Prince of Tides*, a nearly six-hundred-page novel. But the same story was retold powerfully by the novelist and Becky Johnston in a screenplay that was directed brilliantly by Barbra Streisand. When you see the film, you *feel* like you've seen the same story you've read, even though it's "missing" hundreds of pages. This is because the mechanism for telling a story isn't just words. Film needs to use one set of words to create images, novels another, but both have the same framework: they are created with a strong protagonist, a strong antagonist, a conflict, written in scenes that form a three-act structure (with a beginning, middle, and end), and they have a point (theme).

Take this famous Christmastime commercial and break it down:

> Through snowfall, an African-American soldier approaches a cozy-looking house with a lit tree in the window. He starts to ring the doorbell but is greeted by an older man—his father. With fingers to his lips to shush the young soldier, the father lets him in the door and silently embraces him. Then he leads his son to the kitchen, where his mother, back turned to the door, is talking on the phone and baking a pie. The soldier puts his arms around her, and she drops the phone.

It's a powerful story told in sixty seconds with strong characters and a relatable conflict. The structure has three acts: an emotional beginning, a dramatic middle, and a powerful, poignant ending.

Characters—
- The protagonist here is the soldier.
- The antagonist is the separation caused by war, signified by the soldier's uniform.

Conflict—
- War had taken their son away, had altered Christmas.

Scenes—
- Man walking through the snowfall. He approaches the door as Dad opens it. They embrace.
- Dad leads son through their home to the kitchen, where they surprise Mom. She drops the phone and embraces her son.

Structure—
- Soldier (survives war) makes it home—the beginning.
- Dad answers door. He and son are overjoyed—the middle.
- Together, they surprise Mom, for a joyous Christmas after all—the end.

Theme—
- Love conquers all—or in the case of this story, love of family conquers war. And the phone that held them together through it all has done its job.

The characters are defined and developed, complete with **backstory**. There's surprise, anticipation, an **arc**, and a satisfying **resolution**.

In this brief example, we can see all the mechanical ingredients of a successful story.

————————————

As we've noted, stories have a beginning, middle, and end—even though, as French director Jean-Luc Godard remarked, "not necessarily in that order." Life also has a beginning, middle, and end, but by its very nature, we're always "lost at sea" in the middle, living in fear of what the ending might be. For us, it's always too early to define beginnings, too late to judge endings. But we see clearly the shape of a story as we can never see the shape of our own lives. "Count no man happy until he is dead," the ancient Greeks wrote, "The ending is all."

If storytelling imitates reality—while adding a clear ending—we can understand why we so often prefer stories over daily life. Just as nothing can be more tedious than a relative calling to narrate at great length his latest life experiences over the phone, nothing is more soothing to our consciousness than a well-told, well-shaped story.

Think about your friends on Facebook. Many of them use this social media site as a vehicle to share the life and times of their families with the world. We read the same stories over and over. Tyler hit the winning home run. Sheila got all As on her report card. Yet, we look forward to certain people's posts over others because of how they use the vehicle of storytelling to relay information to the world. Perhaps the story of Tyler's home run has a beginning, a middle, and an end—with Ty (our endearing protagonist) striking out two other times, with the team needing three runs to win, with the bases loaded, with Ty recovering from a sprained ankle. *It starts to rain. Is that lightning? Will they stop the game? There are no makeup games in Pee Wee.*

Scintillating stuff. Those are the posts we flock to. Those are the posts we share. Those are the posts we discuss with a mutual friend while sitting at the next sporting event for our kids. Or we share these tales with our own kids that evening at dinner, to inspire them during their next game of the season. If you're like us, you hold onto them for the next time a writer feels stumped or defeated. That's when we use our secret weapon to inspire and reinvigorate—a good, old-fashioned story. We remind our writers what a story is by telling them a story.

Meredith Wild was in technology when she got bit by the proverbial writing bug in 2013. Wild has since had so much success with her digital romance on Amazon that she created her own publishing company, Waterhouse Press, and sold 1.4 million in paperbacks to booksellers like Barnes & Noble, Target, and Walmart. Wild decided to take on other romance authors after that, and will be releasing nine new novels this year, two of which are hers.

3

BREAKING DOWN THE INGREDIENTS TO CONSTRUCT A GREAT STORY

LET'S LOOK AT HOW GREAT storytellers deal with each of the five components to create a great story: character, conflict, scene, structure, theme.

1. *Character:* a protagonist and an antagonist
2. *Conflict:* "What would happen if…?"
3. *Scene:* the **setting** where an action expresses conflict.
4. *Structure:* a beginning, middle, and end—three acts
5. *Theme:* the point—a laugh at the end of a joke, a moral lesson, or a terrifying fright.

1—Character

There *is* no story without strong characters—but don't confuse the characters in your story with human beings. You construct them from human-like parts for the story's dramatic purpose. They are mechanisms, actors in a play designed by you.

All your reader needs to know about your characters is what's required to set the action of your story in motion, and to illustrate the theme of your story. Shakespeare never tells us *why* King Lear comes up with the mind-bending demand that his daughters, Goneril, Regan, and Cordelia, declare to him how much they love him. What if an all-powerful king, at the height of his reign, promises to give his power to the daughter who loves him most? That **premise** is enough to set in motion the **tragic** drama that leads to the protagonist's destruction—and does *not* require deep psychological analysis of Lear's personality defects.

Too much information—the cross we bear daily in our overstimulated lives—is the bane of storytelling.

In a well-told story, all we need is *enough*. "You find the block of marble," as the sculptor Michelangelo Buonarroti explained, and "simply remove everything that is *not* David."

"Enough," when it comes to character, is a protagonist, an antagonist, an **ally** for each, and a love interest for the protagonist. That's about all today's commercial audience can handle unless your reader is stranded on a desert island and has the time and attention span to deal with Leo Tolstoy's *War and Peace*. Tolstoy's classic reappeared on Broadway as a much-abbreviated but still powerful cabaret theater piece, *Natasha, Pierre & the Great Comet of 1812*.

Let's look at the character elements one by one, starting with the most important two characters, the protagonist and the antagonist.

The protagonist, often called "the **hero**" (though he or she doesn't have to be heroic), is the character who performs the primary actions that cause your story's conflict. The story is *about him or her*. By the time the story ends, your audience needs to know what this person is about. In particular, they want to know what her or his **motivation** is all about, what his mission in the story is (Joseph Campbell calls this "the hero's quest"), if and how he changes. That's

23

really all we need to know about him. In the Pet Fish Joke, the hero begins in trouble. He is motivated to get out of trouble. His mission is to get the game warden to give him a chance to get out of trouble. He makes that chance happen with his words. In the words of novelist Vladimir Nabokov, this little joke, like every story, gets the hero up a tree, shakes the tree, then gets him down from the tree in one piece—which is why this one is a **comic** story. If the protagonist had gotten hauled down to the jailhouse with the fish as evidence, it'd be a tragic, unhappy story.

The antagonist is the second most important character in your story, the primary force opposing the protagonist. He is the biggest **obstacle** in the protagonist's attempt to fulfill his mission. The best stories are typically those with the strongest antagonists because the greatest drama comes from pitting two forces against each other. The stronger you make one force, the more the opposite force in your story is tested. Think of Luke Skywalker against Darth Vader, and you understand immediately how a strong antagonist makes a story great. After you have your two main players, the protagonist and the antagonist, fisherman and game warden, if you need more characters to tell your story, you can add:

—Protagonist's ally

—Antagonist's ally

—Love interest for the protagonist

Remember: the best recipe for success when structuring your story is to keep it simple.

Examples of stories with few characters:

- *The Great Gatsby* by F. Scott Fitzgerald
- *Raging Bull* by Mardik Martin & Paul Schraeder
- *The Road* by Cormac McCarthy

- *The Shining* by director Stanley Kubrick & Diane Johnson
- *Annie Hall* by director Woody Allen
- *Who's Afraid of Virginia Woolf?* by Edward Albee
- *Room* by Emma Donoghue
- *Two Girls and a Guy* by James Toback
- *I Am Legend* by Richard Matheson
- *Moonlight* by Barry Jenkins & Tarrell McCraney
- *Before Sunrise* by director Richard Linklater and Kim Krizan
- *Eleanor & Park* by Rainbow Rowell
- *The Designated Mourner* by Mike Nichols
- *The Apartment* by Billy Wilder

2—*Conflict*

Stories are artfully crafted representations of reality, or believable structures, of what might have been, what might be, and what might happen if a character is put into a certain situation or faced with a certain circumstance. Good stories are imbued with conflict.

What would happen if a man like *this* finds himself facing a **crisis** like *that?* We give our protagonist an obstacle to either overcome or be defeated by, and that's how we start creating our story. What would happen if a man fishing out of season was caught by a game warden?

Well-made stories reveal to us the essential form of things—the emotional or dramatic or logical or chronological consequences of action; the causality of behavior; its possible repercussions. What would happen if a woman like *this* discovered herself (because of being the way she is) facing *that?* What would happen if a steelworker moonlighting as an exotic dancer got a chance to audition for a dance troop? Someone longing to pursue his or her dreams can't watch

Flashdance or *La La Land* or *Rocky* or *Billy Elliot* or *Whiplash* or *The Full Monty* or *Slumdog Millionaire* too often. These film stories are fashioned to inspire and motivate, and they draw large audiences because they tap into a longing that's universal.

Don't confuse action and **plot.** Action is about recognizing and embracing your story's natural pattern or shape. It's about character discovery. Focusing too much on a rigid plot—defined as the way the action fits together—can get in the way. The primary principle I use when consulting with students and writers is to help them discover the **mythic substructure** of their stories, the primal pattern that satisfies the audience with the outcome of this kind of character's actions. That's what led us to structure Governor Jesse Ventura's *I Ain't Got Time to Bleed* after the labors of Hercules (who had to perform twelve heroic labors to purify himself), starting with the lead character having to "clean the shit out of the Augean stables."

Let's look at the conflict in *Jerry Maguire,* one of the films Lisa's infatuated with. She's studied this Cameron Crowe Academy Award winner for years. *What would happen if a money-man finds himself facing a crisis of conscience that costs him his career, his fiancée—everything?* The creation of a strong character facing the compelling conflict of losing his career, the love of his life, and the respect of everyone he ever met embarking on a journey to discover what life—true success and genuine love—is supposed to be about, resulted in millions of people lining up for the answer to that simple question: *What would happen if?* The film has made over a quarter of a billion dollars worldwide.

Sliding Doors with Gwyneth Paltrow answers the question of "what might happen if," while juxtaposing it against a second "what might happen if" question that more closely simulates real life. The audience gets to see what happens when Helen arrives home early and catches her boyfriend cheating on her. *What would happen if Helen walks in on her boyfriend in bed with another woman?* Then the movie splits and the audience also gets to experience the "what might happen if" that resembles real life. *What would happen if Helen arrives home ten minutes later, to never learn of her boyfriend's infidelity?* As you can guess, we root for the Helen who caught her man in bed with another woman for the remainder of the show. That's the more dramatic character, the more sympathetic character, the character with the greatest conflict. There's more drama in that story. There's more risk. There's a bigger payoff. Helen has a greater opportunity to grow from the heartbreak, from the truth revealed. *What will she do? Who will she become? After she heals, will she see this an opportunity? And, will she find the one thing we all long for—true love?* If you haven't seen this movie, it's a great example of the differences between "real life," where often the truth isn't revealed, and nothing results, and "great storytelling." Watch this movie and you'll see how you, too, will be rooting for the Helen in the *"What might happen if she caught her boyfriend in bed with another woman"* scenario. This is clear conflict.

Famous stories with clear conflict:

- *The Old Man and the Sea* by Ernest Hemingway—man vs. nature, a fisherman fighting his way back to shore with a legendary catch. Note the same conflict cycled differently in Herman Melville's *Moby-Dick* and Peter Benchley's *Jaws*.
- *Dune* by Frank Herbert—at its core, a story about a young man avenging the death of his father and usurpation of his family by powerful villains. This is an example of a story with a complex world but simple through line.
- *Night* by Elie Wiesel—a young Jewish boy's struggle to survive Nazi concentration camps.
- *The Godfather* by Mario Puzo—Can Michael Corleone transcend his father's mafia family? Son vs. father.

- *Brokeback Mountain* by Annie Proulx—two young men with otherwise separate lives discover their attraction to each other in 1963 Wyoming. Love vs. acceptance in society.
- *The Meg* from the novel by Steve Alten—man against a humongous shark.
- *The Martian* by Andy Weir (originally direct-published)—What would happen if one man was left behind in the inhospitable environment of Mars?
- *Holes* by Louis Sachar—A middle schooler is unjustly sentenced to a juvenile correctional camp because of a family curse.
- *Dunkirk* by Christopher Nolan—Allies vs. Nazis.
- *Girl on the Train* by Paula Hawkins—What might happen if a passenger watching events unfold from the safety of her train compartment gets off the train and gets involved in the lives she's spied on.
- *Groundhog Day* by Harold Ramis and Danny Rubin—one man against a time loop.

We gave notes to a writer once about a lack of conflict in her young adult fantasy story. She said she had decided not to have her two leads (protagonists) ever get together in the story because "everybody does that." She thought it'd be interesting if her characters were more like real life, where sometimes nothing ever happens. Joseph Heller's *Something Happened* was once brutally panned in two words: "Nothing happened." Must there be romance to propel a plot? No. Must there be conflict with growth, change, some kind of awakening? Yes. Even in *Sleepless in Seattle,* the characters come together at the end. Unfortunately, not only romance but an awakening/growth/change was absent from her novel, too. Sometimes romance sounds like a cop-out—too easy. But when writers are starting out, are new to structure, and want commercial success, romance is a handy tool for relatability. Fiction fans aren't interested in reading about "real life," or reading about characters that "nothing happens to." In life, we're lost at sea somewhere in the middle because we're either too young to appreciate our beginnings or too dead to judge our endings. In life, we often meet someone we're attracted to, but nothing ever happens. These aren't situations that turn into famous stories that we recap for years to come to our children and grandchildren. The great stories are about great loves and epic losses, the people with whom we connected for better or for worse.

3—Scene

The scene is the unit of drama, the stage within the stage where conflict occurs between the characters. **Paragraphs**, **chapters**, sections, parts are also measurements, but none of them can perform the structural service of the scene.

Great writers don't write pages, they write scenes. Like the story itself, a scene

1. is set in a certain place; important to dramatizing the story;
2. has a beginning, middle, and end. The beginning hooks the protagonist—and, you, reader or audience—into the scene. The middle complicates things for the protagonist. The end gets her out of the scene, happily or not, and preferably in a cliffhanging way that hooks you into continuing the story.
3. is the place where conflict occurs, so a scene without conflict needs to be either *conflicted* or edited out. And, once the conflict is shown and resolved (or shown to have created more complications), the scene is over.

Reminder: stories are written not page by page, but scene by scene.

The length of a scene is a function of a given writer's style, his or her signature: Kurt Vonnegut loves short, telegraphic scenes; William Faulkner was known for his long and lumbering scenes that can last page after page after page. Regardless of length, the scene must get the job done, and the job is to:

1. place the character in a situation, consisting of a setting and an obstacle.
2. make the character deal with the obstacle.
3. extract the character from the situation, preferably with a hook into his next scene.

Each scene reiterates the overall structure Nabokov was talking about when he told storytellers to get your hero up a tree, shake the tree, then get him down from the tree. One of the magical secrets of good storytelling is that the storyteller has a knack for treating the *units* of the story, the *scenes,* as though each is as important as the overall story. That's what Dante Alighieri meant when he wrote that "the part must reflect the whole." *Scenes are the link in the chain that is your story.*

You'll find your daily writing discipline much easier to maintain if you set yourself the goal of writing in scenes instead of pages. A. E. Van Vogt, iconic sci-fi author of the twentieth century with over 300 titles to his credit, told me that his day's work was done when he'd written a scene. Then he could go off and do whatever he felt like doing, confident that the *next scene* would be percolating in the back of his mind until tomorrow.

Here are excerpts from the opening pages (the **set-up**) in C. S. Lewis's *The Lion, the Witch and the Wardrobe*—a solid demonstration of great scene building.

Set-up—

Once there were four children whose names were Peter, Susan, Edmund and Lucy. This story is about something that happened to them when they were sent away from London [to an old Professor's house] during the war because of air-raids. (Page 1)

—————————————————————

As soon as they said goodnight to the Professor and gone upstairs on the first night, the boys came into the girls' room and they all talked it over. (Page 2)

—————————————————————

But when next morning came, there was steady rain falling, so thick that when you looked out of the window you could see neither the mountains nor the woods nor even the stream in the garden.

"Of course, it would be raining!" said Edmund.

(Pages 3 and 4)

"Not for me," said Peter. "I'm going to explore the house."

Everyone agreed to this and that was how the adventures began. (Page 4)

Scene—

1. **Place** the character(s) in a situation/setting with an obstacle.

"Nothing here!" said Peter, [of one of the bedrooms] and they all trooped out again, except for Lucy. (Page 5)

2. **Make** the character deal with the obstacle.

...Looking into the inside [of the wardrobe] she saw several coats hanging up—mostly long fur coats. ...She immediately stepped inside...leaving the door open, of course, because she knew that it is very foolish to shut oneself into any wardrobe. ...She took a step further in— then two or three steps—always expecting to feel the woodwork against the tips of her fingers. But she could not feel it. (Pages 5 and 6)

3. **Extract** the character from the situation, preferably with a hook into the next scene.

The next moment she found that what was rubbing against her face and hands was no longer soft fur but something hard and rough and even prickly. "Why, it is just like the branches of a tree!" exclaimed Lucy. (Bottom of Page 6)

The book opens with the children being sent to the home of a stranger. By morning, due to heavy rain, they can't go play outside like kids do, so they decide to explore the house. The scene that sets the stage for the whole story (their journey to Narnia) starts with Lucy staying behind in a room because the wardrobe has her curious. (1. Lucy is placed in the setting—the room with the wardrobe.) To her surprise it's not locked, and she goes in to feel and smell the luxurious fur coats hanging inside. She doesn't shut the wardrobe doors, as even a child knows that would be foolish. (2. Lucy is made to "deal with the obstacle" by going inside the wardrobe.) But as she steps in farther, she finds there's no "back" to this wardrobe, and she steps and steps until she comes out the other side, where there are tree branches brushing her cheeks and snow dampening her hair. She's in the land of Narnia. (3. Lucy is extracted from this scene, making it complete, and there's a hook into the next scene—as she walks into the land of Narnia.)

C. S. Lewis uses the three steps of effective scene writing to complete his set-up and propel us into the "middle of the book," and he accomplishes this in six short pages. This is as literal and effective as it gets—a clear-cut demonstration how scenes carry a story from one moment to the next, how characters are the tools used to take us there, and how the words play the most minor role of all.

It's books like these that we should read and re-read when learning how to get from Stage 1 to Stage 2 in our growth as a writer.

Another scene I love is from *Hook's Tale, Being the Account of an Unjustly Villainized Pirate Written by Himself,* emended and edited by John Leonard Pielmeier, copyright 2017 by John Pielmeier, published by Scribner, an imprint of Simon and Schuster, Inc. Here it is along with John's introduction:

> James Hook, aged fourteen and an orphan, has found himself transported from England to a mysterious tropical archipelago where Time seems to behave quite differently from what he's used to. His life is saved by a flying boy named Peter who lives on an island called the Never-isle, and (after a swim with some voluptuous mermaids) Peter takes him to visit a tribe of people living in a village of tents on an island promontory. There Hook meets Panther, the tribal chief (and a collector of beautiful seashells), Panther's

lovely daughter Tiger Lily, and Lone Wolf, Tiger Lily's fiancé. Tiger Lily, due to a regrettable promise made by her father, is to be sacrificed on the morrow to The-Great-God-Below-Who-Is-Death, a mysterious creature living at the bottom of a deep well. Late that night Hook retires to the lip of the promontory to study the stars and to contemplate the meaning of Death.

Hook's Tale is very much a book about the process of aging, and the reason I love this scene is that it illustrates the first step our hero takes toward maturation.

Scene—

"It's a gorgeous night, isn't it?" asked a voice behind me.

I turned around and saw a slim figure silhouetted against the campfires of the village. It was the Princess Tiger Lily.

"May I join you?" she asked.

"Please, yes, I would be honored," I said and shifted to make room. She allowed her legs to dangle over the high cliff.

"You're Peter's new friend," she declared.

"Yes. I'm James, your Highness. He saved my life." I instantly worried that my mention of "life" would stir unhappy thoughts in her.

"He's a brave boy with a good heart," she said. "He's at times too much of a boy. He's always entertaining, but he doesn't know how to handle—well—other emotions very well. He was afraid to say goodbye to me."

She sounded like a woman of wisdom, of careful observation learned from the experience of a long life. This, of course, was probably true; she may have been even older than Peter, in Never-isle terms. But it was the "womanness" of her wisdom that struck a chord within me. My mother, at her best, might say things like this; still, there was a heat in Tiger Lily's words that made me aware of things about her that went beyond mothering. She wasn't as delightfully womanly as the mermaids, of course, but still she stirred something within me, something that superseded mere affection.

"I'm glad you came with him," she added.

"Why? I'm a stranger."

"But you're new to this world, aren't you?"

I nodded.

"I like that. There's something about you that still sees things. Too many people here—mostly the men and boys—forget that there is more to life than just the Now. For that I'm glad of my leaving. My father and Lone Wolf and most of the males in the tribe are suddenly thinking about things they don't usually pay the least bit of attention to. Even with all that, they're sleeping soundly tonight, dreaming of food or the hunt or some new adventure. No one is taking the moment to look at the stars and think about what it all might mean. Like you."

"But I don't know what it all might mean. Nor do I understand why your father doesn't simply say no. Toss a few shells to The-Great-God or whatever it is and be done with it."

"He's given his word. That is more precious to him even than I am. And I must say I'm proud of him for that."

"But you could run away, couldn't you? And there's nothing your father could do about it. If you weren't available and the God still demanded something precious, he might still hand over a very nice shell."

She smiled. "Thank you, James. That's a very clever solution. But I'm a little too duty-bound for my own good, I admit. I don't think I could live with myself if I ran away from the village. I could certainly never face Father again, not to mention Lone Wolf."

"But if they love you, don't they want you alive, Princess?"

"Life is no condition for Loving, James. More often than not it makes Loving more complicated. And vice versa."

I thought about this for a moment. It made me sad. The person I loved the most, until now, was my mother, and it wasn't easy keeping her in mind nearly every moment of every day. I worried that if loving a living someone was more of a challenge, how could I ever manage it? I didn't like to think about this, and so I changed the subject.

"Are you afraid, Princess? Of dying?"

"A little. I try to think of it as Curiosity more than Fear. I like adventure too, and Death will be an awfully big one."

In the silence that followed I studied her face. Desperate, I plumbed for Hope.

"You're going to descend into something called the Deep Well, yes?"

She nodded.

"Are you sure there's a god down there? 'Who-Is-Death?' I mean, maybe there's nothing. Maybe you'll spend a damp morning in the well and then you'll simply come back up."

"No one who's descended in the past has ever returned. We-Who-Are-Above listen, and we hear screams, and sometimes a great roar, and then there's silence again. Granted, most of the Voluntary Descents tend to be old people or the occasional Disappointed Lover, so there's little expectation for a triumphant return. We did send the Great White Father down, but we don't like to speak of that."

"The Great White Father? Who's that?"

"We don't like to speak of it, James," she sternly reminded me. "Besides, he didn't return either, which was all for the best."

"Still, whatever is down there may not be immortal."

"It's always been there, at least according to the songs. They used to toss people down, on occasion, to make The-God happy, but even when they did he never laughed, so I don't think happiness was an achievable outcome. Anyway, they stopped doing that long ago. They just pray now, and on occasion throw him a few rutabagas."

"But if he—or it—is mortal, it could be conquered. Why doesn't someone go down with you? Lone Wolf—he looks like a proper warrior. He could fight the God, and perhaps even kill him. And then you and he could live happily ever after. Or something like that."

"Yes, I've wondered about that too, but you see—" She stopped, as if she knew a secret she was afraid to spill. "I shouldn't say."

"What? I won't tell."

She took a deep breath, then sighed. "Lone Wolf is afraid," she whispered. "As is my father. As are all the men.

Even Peter. They're all afraid of The-Great-God-Below-Who-Is-Death."

"But being afraid shouldn't stop anyone. I mean we're all afraid of Death. I certainly am."

"Yes, but they're also afraid to admit it. Anyway, they won't go down. I'll have a bow and a quiver of arrows with me, and I'm a very good shot, so there's some hope."

I looked away for a time, studying the lowest star. Then I took her hand.

"I'll go with you."

Tears sprang to her eyes, and I knew right away that, even if it ended badly, this was the best and bravest decision I had ever made in my short life.

Pielmeier introduces his protagonist to a new dramatic element, Tiger Lily, and develops a relationship between protagonist and ally that quickly becomes complicated and conflicted, including an occasional **tunneling** into backstory that serves to accentuate the conflict. The scene ends in a resolution—that Hook will accompany Tiger Lily in her descent into darkness—that also serves as an excellent hook into the next scene.

4—*Structure*

Breaking Down the Beginning, Middle, End

A strong story has strong characters, a compelling conflict, and a discernible beginning, middle, and end. Yes, we keep reiterating this. It's vital to understand the difference between real life and a great story before you enter Stage 2 of a writer's journey to tell the story that's been keeping you awake at night.

Beginning (a.k.a. "set-up" a.k.a. "Act 1")

A masterful beginning hooks the reader—your eyes widen as you read the rest of the first page, and you can't help but turn to the second page. You are hooked, addicted, and there's no way out but through the story. There's no other feeling like this. You need to immerse yourself in the world of this story, you need to experience it, and then you need to tell everyone you know, so they can experience it, too. This is what the beginning of a great story feels like.

A story's beginning has but one purpose: to lure the reader or audience into the storyteller's spell. The opening has nothing to do with logic, and certainly not with chronology. Life may begin with the mundane trauma of birth on a cold winter day, but a story begins with the storyteller capturing the audience's full attention. It's not complicated; as Stephen King says: "An opening line should invite the reader to begin the story. It should say: Listen. Come in here. You want to know about this." Here are a few classic openings.

Five Beginnings That Hook

- *Beholding Bee* by Kimberly Newton Fusco (Young Adult)

> The way I got the diamond on my face happened like this.
>
> I was sleeping in the back of our hauling truck one night after Pauline shut down our hot dog cart and Ellis closed the merry-go-round and the Ferris wheel, and then, after every one of the stars had blinked out for the night so no one could see, that is when an angel came and kissed me on the cheek.
>
> That is the way Pauline sees it.

Other folks say different things, like "What a shame, what a shame." I hear them when I am chopping onions and Pauline is frying hot dogs. "Now there's a heavy load for a little slip of a thing to carry." They make it sound like I am lugging coal.

• *The Bridges of Madison County* by Robert James Waller (Romance)

There are songs that come free from the blue-eyed grass, from the dust of a thousand country roads. This is one of them.

• *The Glass Castle* by Jeannette Walls (Memoir)

I was sitting in a taxi, wondering if I had overdressed for the evening, when I looked out the window and saw Mom rooting through a Dumpster. It was just after dark. A blustery March wind whipped the steam coming out of the manholes, and people hurried along the sidewalks with their collars turned up. I was stuck in traffic two blocks from the party where I was heading.

• *Nobody Walks* by Dennis M. Walsh (True Crime Story)

Sometimes life deals a hand you may not be prepared to play. When my younger brother was murdered, it quickly became obvious that many potential witnesses were either afraid to cooperate with the police or didn't want to be considered rats, or both. My brother's murder was not about to become a cold case, not if I could help it. This was a hand I thought I could play.

- *Watchers* by Dean Koontz

On this thirty-sixth birthday, May 18, Travis Cornell rose at five o'clock in the morning. He dressed in sturdy hiking boots, jeans, and a long-sleeved, blue-plaid cotton shirt. He drove his pickup south from his home in Santa Barbara all the way to rural Santiago Canyon on the eastern edge of Orange County, south of Los Angeles. He took only a package of Oreo cookies, a large canteen of orange-flavored Kool-Aid, and a fully loaded Smith & Wesson .38 Chief's Special.

During the two-and-a-half-hour trip, he never switched on the radio. He never hummed, whistled, or sang to himself as men alone frequently do. For part of the drive, the Pacific lay on his right. The morning sea was broodingly dark toward the horizon, as hard and cold as slate, but nearer shore it was brightly spangled with early light the colors of pennies and rose petals. Travis did not once glance in appreciatively at the sun-sequined water.

- *A Fine and Private Place* by Peter S. Beagle (Comic Novel)

The baloney weighed the raven down, and the shopkeeper almost caught him as he whisked out the delicatessen door. Frantically he beat his wings to gain altitude, looking like a small black electric fan. An updraft caught him and threw him into the sky. He circled twice, to get his bearings, and fly north.

41

Below, the shopkeeper stood with his hands on his hips, looking up at the diminishing cinder in the sky. Presently he shrugged and went back into his delicatessen. He was not without philosophy, this shopkeeper, and he knew that if a raven comes into your delicatessen and steals a whole baloney it is either an act of God or it isn't, and in either case there isn't very much you can do about it....

There are as many great beginnings as there are great storytellers. One draws you into the story through curiosity alone (as just demonstrated in Dean Koontz's *Watchers*—a man leaving on a trip with Oreos, Kool-Aide, and a loaded gun). Another opening wins your empathy for the narrator (the adolescent girl with the scar on her face in *Beholding Bee* by Kimberly Newton Fusco); yet, another hooks you through voyeuristic shock (the protagonist seeing her homeless mother digging in a dumpster on her way to a NYC gala in *The Glass Castle* by Jeannette Walls). If you're turning the page, you've fallen into the storyteller's spell—which is why the beginning of a story is often referred to as "the hook."

Some beginnings, like the first lines of Charles Dickens's *A Tale of Two Cities*, are more literary, but equally unforgettable. Dickens hooks us with mood and setting:

It was the best of times, it was the worst of times; it was the age of wisdom, it was the age of foolishness; it was the epoch of belief, it was the epoch of incredulity; it was the season of Light, it was the season of Darkness; it was the spring of hope, it was the winter of despair; we had everything before us, we had nothing before us; we were all going directly to Heaven, we were all going the other way.

Whatever you must do to get our attention, do it immediately. Grab us by the throat. Tell us, one way or another, "The pages you are about to read will change your life."

From its opening, the beginning of your story goes on to (a) **establish** the protagonist (sometimes called the "hero"); (b) establish a forward direction for him or her that gives the reader a glimpse into his or her mission or purpose ("the hero's quest"); (c) establish the antagonist in the story who will become the protagonist's obstacle and must therefore be in every sense as powerful as he is; and (d) bring them together in a scene that turns the protagonist away from his initial mission in an unexpected direction that will be the story you're telling. This unexpected move is often called a **reversal**. Once your protagonist starts moving in that new direction, we've entered the middle of the story (also known as Act 2).

Middle (Act 2)

It's the "going on" that causes the storyteller the most sweat and tears. In *A Writer's Time,* I refer to the middle of a story as the Serengeti Plain because it's the most arduous journey the novelist ever undertakes. Great beginnings are relatively easy to drum up. Even endings are a piece of cake compared to the part of the book that must, after all, encompass eighty to ninety percent of your story. Just as some joke tellers are good only with short jokes, hopelessly boggling the longer ones, many writers are brilliant at beginnings and endings but become bogged down in the middle. The ability to construct a middle to your story—whether it's a novel, a screenplay, or even a short story—will separate you from those who haven't been able to crack the high-rolling world of commercial storytelling. If you're wondering about guidelines for the middle of your story, that part is simple:

1. The set-up is complete when the reader or audience is hooked.
2. The middle of your story begins when the set-up is complete.
3. The middle ends when you've brought your characters to the **climax** point, which is the scene in the story where all the conflicts introduced throughout reach a scene in which they're resolved one way or another.

Between set-up and climax lies the steppes of Central Asia—the seemingly endless territory that starts around page twenty or thirty of a screenplay and ends around to page eighty or so (of a 100-page script). The steppes can begin somewhere between pages two and fifty of a novel and end fifty pages or fewer from the last page of the book. What happens in the well-developed middle to keep an audience or reader moving forward includes obstacles, **cliffhangers**, twists, turning points, surprises, chills, scares, and anything else you can imagine that shapes the trek across the steppes into a rollercoaster ride to keep your audience as hooked as they were by your beginning.

The key to a good rollercoaster ride is an unpredictable rhythm of ups and downs. We know, in a romantic comedy, that boy and girl will have obstacles after they meet at the beginning and will wind up together at the end. The accomplished storyteller manages to make the obstacles unexpected and their resolution surprising.

Five Books with Great Middles

- *The Firm* by John Grisham—conflict builds to greater and greater extremes as the story progresses.

- *The Time Traveler's Wife* by Audrey Niffenegger—due to the main character being a time traveler, there is no way of knowing which moment of the relationship will come next.
- *The Curious Incident of the Dog in the Night-Time* by Mark Haddon—the narrator's perspective on solving a mysterious death and his unique experience with the mundane world around him makes it anything but.
- *American Gods* by Neil Gaitan—the protagonist travels across the US and continues to struggle with a more bizarre world than he ever imagined possible.
- *Thirteen Reasons Why* by Jay Asher—We know the outcome of this tragic novel—the end—but the reveal continues to build throughout the middle, shocking us and breaking our hearts at every turn.

Here's an exercise to make sure you have a strong middle:

1. Jot down a single line to describe the scenes in the middle of your story.
2. Rate each line on an **intensity** scale of 1–10.
3. Now, on a clean sheet of paper, represent each scene by drawing a shorter or longer line, depending on the intensity number next to it. Intensity 1 is represented by a single hyphen; 2 by two hyphens, etc.
4. Rotate this page to the left. You now have a physical chart/graph of your rollercoaster middle.

Lost in the Sun by Lisa Graff

The story opens (begins) with—

Trent, our protagonist, is twelve and about to start the sixth grade. He's sitting in a park doodling in "his book of thoughts," and watching some peers play baseball. Trent loves baseball but isn't playing, which we find odd, even though we don't know why he's not playing. Another girl, Fallon, plays in another part of the park. Trent is a kid with the weight of the world on his shoulders. (We don't know the reason for that either, yet.) A baseball rolls his way. He stares at it. Kids yell at him for the ball. Then they ridicule him, then they ridicule his sketchbook and try to see his drawings. This is when Fallon steps in and saves him by covering for him and his sketches. By the end of this opening chapter/scene, Trent reveals through first-person narration that six months ago, in February, while playing pickup hockey, an accident resulted in the death of a peer, which Trent reveals to us by stating, "That was the day I killed Jared Richards." This "event," in the case of this story, is the antagonist. Trent's book of thoughts is sketches of all the different ways Jared could have died, had Trent "not killed him." It is this event that Trent must face and overcome if he is to survive the sixth grade and the rest of his life. And he has no idea how to do that.

With the set-up (beginning) complete, here is our middle—

1. Trent goes to school feeling paranoid and with a chip on his shoulder. He knocks a plant over with his elbow in Mrs. Emerson's homeroom and refuses to participate in gym.

    — — —

2. Trent has a nice lunch with Fallon, even though she's weird and keeps making up fantastical stories about how she got the big scar that extends diagonally across her entire face.

    —

3. Trent meets his dad and his new wife for dinner with his older brother, Aaron, and younger brother, Doug. There's tension.

— —

4. Trent refuses to participate in gym all week. Mrs. Emerson finally warns him that he will flunk the sixth grade if he flunks gym.

— — — —

5. Trent refuses to show Fallon his book of thoughts after she's repeatedly asked.

— — — — —

6. Trent picks a fight and skips out during dinner with Dad.

— — — — — —

7. Fallon starts a movie club at her house after school. Baseball movies. Trent is in.

—

8. Trent spends the weekend at Dad's, visiting the new baby. They don't let him hold her, and he loses it big time.

— — — — — — — — —

9. Trent goes to the lake and tosses one of his books of thoughts into it. This brings him some relief.

— —

10. The gym teacher gives Trent an ultimatum—join intramural baseball, or coach little kids on Saturdays (basketball), in exchange for passing gym.

— — — —

11. Fallon invites Trent (and only Trent) to her birthday party. They go to the local fair.

—

12. Trent sees his mom's boss, Ray, kiss her, and he becomes very angry.

— — — — —

13. Trent chooses basketball and goes to his first practice. There, he is partnered with Annie Richards, the little sister of the kid he accidentally killed. She tells him she hates him.

    — — — — — — — —

14. Trent and Fallon go to the movies. Trent beats up bully Jeremiah after he makes fun of Fallon's scar.

    — — — — — — — — —

15. Fallon runs to Trent's mom's place of work and hides in the back.

    — — — — — — — —

16. She finally lets Trent in, but he doesn't understand why sticking up for her was so wrong and why she's devastated. Fallon confesses that sometimes she has nightmares—and she can't scream. She's lost her scream.

    — — — — — — —

17. Fallon doesn't respond to Trent at lunch. Also, she cancels movie club for good.

    — — — — — — — —

18. Mom tells Trent he needs to live with Dad, but she calls him in front of Trent and he says no.

    — — — — — — — — — —

19. Trent looks for Fallon at Mrs. Emerson's after school and ends up confessing that Fallon is very angry with him. Mrs. Emerson tells him that he needs to figure out how to gain her trust again and he needs to speak in "truths." Mrs. Emerson adds that Trent can water her plants every day after school. He agrees to this.

    —

20. Trent goes to basketball. Annie decides to stay partners with him, even after given the opportunity to switch.

    — — —

21. Mom takes Trent to the movies, where he apologizes to Jeremiah for punching him.

— —

22. Trent goes to Fallon's father and tells him that he will do anything so he can be trusted and hang out with Fallon again. He speaks in "truths." Fallon's dad reluctantly lets Trent in for dinner, but then tells Trent that he's "not the person" he needs to convince of that.

— — — —

23. Doug, Trent's little brother, confesses to Trent that it's all his fault Jared is dead because he told Trent about the pickup truck.

— —

24. Trent finally shows Fallon his book of thoughts—it's all drawings of her fantastical stories about the scar on her face.

— —

25. Trent confronts Mom about lying about Ray.

— — —

26. Trent, with the help of Aaron, takes Fallon to an island by the local beach, where he tells her they are going to "scream." She screams a scream that has been trapped inside her since her face was slashed. Trent joins her, then they fall on the beach exhausted and laughing…and finally free.

—

The dashes track the INTENSITY RATING—represent the dramatic climb. Once you rotate the chart to the left, you can see the drama building, then being resolved, then mounting and building and not resolving, until it climaxes, and the main conflict finds resolution. Our protagonist triumphs over the antagonist in this case, as this story has a happy ending.

Note: the rollercoaster, or lack thereof, is visible when you simply rotate the chart. The chart will allow you to shift the scenes around if need be. You can intensify or de-intensify them, to create a rhythmic pattern of rising and falling action caused by your protagonist's encounter with obstacles that he either overcomes or is defeated by. This is how you hold your audience's attention.

Once you've brought the protagonist to the ultimate obstacle, where the antagonist has rallied his greatest strength, sometimes against the protagonist's weakest moment, you've reached Act 3, or the ending of your story.

End (Act 3)

The ending of a well-made story fulfills the storyteller's obligation to satisfy the audience's expectations for a conclusive ending, whether happy—where the protagonist overcomes the ultimate obstacle and goes on with his new life—or tragic—where the protagonist is defeated, even killed. Gabriel García Márquez's *Love in the Time of Cholera* ends with the frustrated lovers finally uniting after a lifetime of separation. Judith Rossner's *Looking for Mr. Goodbar* ends with the protagonist's murder. In both cases, the reader feels the impact of a well-told story, moved to joy by García Márquez, to horror by Rossner. In R. J. Palacio's 2014 release, *Wonder*, she heals the readers' hearts with a solid ending. After being ridiculed and isolated through the entire fifth-grade school year, Augie, a boy born with a severe facial deformity, finds himself off school grounds getting beaten up by random bigger kids who hate him for how he looks. This is when some other boys—who've bullied and/or ignored him all year—step in, helping Auggie defend himself. Augie goes home a bruised and bloodied mess. But he goes back to school a new person. The "mean" kids from school had stuck up for him. He's no longer alone. Thanks to the physical pain of the brawl, hope, friendship, and love are born. He is healed. The kids at school are healed from the fight, too. Augie is now accepted, and the mean kids are no longer mean, for they've realized the error of their ways. Endings like these give us all hope; they make us believe in miracles. Julia Roberts and Owen Wilson star in the film, a Lionsgate production, released in the fall of 2017.

Your story's ending should be conclusive, dramatic, satisfying. It should not be indefinite, cerebral, or too abrupt—leave that for the academics. Readers and audience members feel like they deserve a definite ending that leaves them weeping or happy.

Stories with Effective Endings

- *Fight Club* by Chuck Palahniuk
- *Moby-Dick* by Herman Melville
- *Charlotte's Web* by E.B. White
- Peter Weir's *Witness*
- *The Kite Runner* by Khaled Hosseini
- M. Night Shyamalan's *The Sixth Sense*
- *The Book Thief* by Markus Zusak
- Billy Wilder's *Some Like It Hot*
- *The Great Gatsby* by F. Scott Fitzgerald

5—*Premise & Theme*

A story is a mechanism structured in scenes that show characters in accelerating conflict with a beginning, a middle, and climactic end.

We use thousands of words to tell our story. But our story should be so well-constructed that it can be explained in one line—called the premise.

Premises are specific. You can say, "The story is about...." Or you can put it into our "what if" formula. A great story creates conflict and ultimately resolution that asks and answers the question: *What would happen if a character like THIS faces a crisis like THAT? What happens if a sometime sailor faces the mightiest monster the sea has ever created? (Moby-Dick, The Old Man and the Sea, The Hunter and the Whale, Jaws).*

The premise is the reason for telling the story.

The theme is revealed once we know how the story ends: "You can't beat Mother Nature" or, better: "If you want the ultimate test, go against Mother Nature." The latter formulation suggests that the premise of *Jaws* and *The Martian* are identical; only the setting and story details are different. We *love* premises because they are life's most enduring lessons; we never tire of seeing them reenacted. They may help us in our personal struggles.

Here's a list of five books and their premises (so you understand the importance of a clearly-defined premise):

- *White Oleander* by Janet Fitch—the effects of the foster care system on an adolescent girl after her mother is sent to prison.
- *Perks of Being a Wallflower* by Stephen Chbosky—a socially awkward teen must find self-confidence and learn to fit in after his only friends leave for college.
- Harry Potter series by J. K. Rowling—boy wizard goes to a magic school and must fight for his life against the dark lord who murdered his parents.

- *The Art of Racing in the Rain* by Garth Stein—an intimate look at a family's dynamics as seen through the eyes of their dog.
- *The Leftovers* by Tom Perrotta—a group of New Yorkers must struggle to survive after the unexplained disappearance of a large part of the world's population.

More examples of dramatic premises:

- *What would happen if a man set out to compare the love of his three daughters?* This is the premise behind William Shakespeare's tragedy *King Lear*.
- *What would happen if a suicidal homicide detective was partnered with a cop just trying to survive a few more months until retirement?* That's the "what if" behind *Lethal Weapon*.
- *What would happen if an ambitious jazz student was placed under the tutelage of a brilliant but sadistic instructor?* That's the premise of the Academy-award winning indie film *Whiplash*.
- *What would happen if a down-on-his-luck theater owner held a singing competition with a cash prize larger than he could produce to save the business?* That's the premise of *Sing*, the animated musical comedy produced by Illumination Entertainment.

Notice that the premise of an effective story contains the seeds of conflict. Having a contest of loyalties among three women, siblings or not, is asking for trouble. In *Lethal Weapon*, partnering an unstable cop with a suicide wish with one that wants to fly under the radar until retirement is asking for conflict (and comedy). In *Whiplash*, you have two overachievers, except one—the teacher—doesn't have boundaries. The conflict is about who will break first. In *Sing*, the solution to saving the theater—a contest with a cash prize—creates an even more massive conflict, because it becomes a newsworthy story and still there's no money—for the winner or to save the theatre.

If you don't quite know your premise as you're writing your story's first draft, that's okay. But you can't *edit* your story without figuring it out. How would you know what to cut and what to keep? You wouldn't.

An effective story comes from a premise that gives rise to conflict. In resolving the conflict, the storyteller discovers the theme.

Themes are universal, rooted in the common myths of humanity. You can read different books and see vastly different movies with the same themes and not even realize it, due to the characters and settings being so different.

Here are a few examples of different books and movies with similar themes:

- *Sense and Sensibility* (Jane Austen) and *Bridget Jones's Diary* (Helen Fielding)—what we're willing to sacrifice for love.
- *Of Mice and Men* (John Steinbeck) and *About a Boy* (Nick Hornby)—the pathos of isolation.
- *The Wolf of Wall Street* (Jordan Belfort) and *Frankenstein* (Mary Shelley)—misuse of knowledge and power leads to destruction of yourself and those around you.
- *Lethal Weapon* (Shane Black) and *Planes, Trains and Automobiles* (John Hughes)—don't judge others until you've walked in their shoes.
- *The English Patient* (Michael Ondaatje) and *The Other Woman* (Don Ross, based on Ayelet Waldman's *Love and Other Impossible Pursuits*)—no good comes to the unfaithful.

- *Field of Dreams* (Phil Alden Robinson, based on *Shoeless Joe* by W.P. Kinsella) and *August Rush* (based on a story by Nick Castle)—build it (play it) and they will come.
- William Shakespeare's *Macbeth,* Arthur Miller's *Death of a Salesman,* Oliver Stone's *Wall Street,* Martin Scorsese's *Casino* (based on the novel by Nicholas Pileggi), and Robert Klane's *Weekend at Bernie's*—overwhelming greed and ambition will inevitably destroy everything around it, including the greedy person.

Examining themes is further proof that stories are not built on words but on structure. How else could we compare Shakespeare, Miller, and Scorsese's work to Robert Klane's comedy *Weekend at Bernie's?* Their stories were all built on the same themes, the same structure, the same conflict, further emphasizing that a story is not about its words.

Your story's *plot* is simply the linking together of all the dramatic elements in a way that makes your story seamlessly believable, that allows it to flow into the audience's consciousness without drawing attention to any of the parts.

When you achieve that seamless communication, your tale is well spun.

Michael J. Sullivan spent more than a decade studying Stephen King, Ernest Hemingway, and John Steinbeck, during which time he wrote thirteen novels that never found homes with a traditional publisher. He stopped writing for ten years until a new series began to brew inside him. When he started writing again, his wife jumped on board to assist in direct publishing. Between 2008 and 2010, five of his Riyria Revelation fantasy novels were direct-published and/or released through a small press publication. He has sold nearly a million copies of his books to date and has spent three-plus years on the Amazon Bestselling Fantasy Author's list. He has eleven books in circulation, five on the way. Michael utilizes direct publishing, boutique press, and traditional publishing simultaneously to maximize his success. But remember: he found success first in the world of self-publishing.

4

WHAT MAKES A GREAT STORYTELLER?

NOW YOU KNOW WHAT A story is. It is a *structure* of three acts that are further broken down into *scenes*, with a premise and a *theme*, showing *characters*—a protagonist and an antagonist—that endure *conflict* (twists, turns, and reversals) until a satisfying resolution—the end—is reached.

Now let's look at what makes a story *great* and a storyteller *great*.

Getting your story across in business, relationships, politics, as well as in commercial storytelling, is as important a craft as structuring the story itself. What professors and critics call "classic literature" is commercial literature that has survived through the ages.

Great commercial storytellers have a knack for accomplishing this without drawing attention to themselves. Aristotle, in his *Poetics* manual of storytelling, remarked that Homer's greatness was that "he himself is nowhere to be found in his works. His characters are everywhere." The same could be said of Shakespeare, the master of "show, don't tell." Mark Twain put it this way: "Don't say the old lady screamed—bring her on and let her scream." That's what editors mean when they say, "Show, don't tell." Showing *involves* while telling *distances* the reader.

The most important lessons you might ever learn about effective storytelling are:

1. *It's not about you.*
2. *It's not about your characters.*
3. *It's not even about the words.*
4. *It's about your reader, the audience.*

How can my story not be about me? I wrote the damn thing. I lived it! I mean, I altered it to have a happy ending, of course, but it's my story. Mine!

Not if you're interested in commercial success, it's not. Remember Aristotle's observation about Homer's greatness: "He himself is nowhere to be found in his work. His characters are everywhere."

"Write drunk, edit sober." Hemingway was right on the money. A drunk person has no mental filter, so write that first draft without filtering yourself. Let some time pass, then bring out your inner editor and filter your work, sobering up your sloppy—but honest—storytelling. If you don't enjoy Hemingway's method, you can still "write drunk" and "edit sober" by writing your story to the best of your ability then finding a kickass editor to take it from there. This is what professional storytellers do. Your story isn't even written by you—Jill the lawyer, Joe the construction worker, Joe the tech support guy. It's written by "Jill the author." Few authors have made this clearer than Lemony Snicket, the author of the *A Series of Unfortunate Events* novels turned movie, TV series, and video game. Lemony Snicket is the pen name of writer/musician/journalist Daniel Handler. Handler—the musician, journalist, husband, and father—understands that he is not the author of his books. In fact, he created a whole world in which the author of his books, Lemony Snicket, lives and breathes, even making him a widower.

Okay, I think I can understand that: you don't want my opinion to tarnish or affect my story or to influence the characters living it. Got it. But, how can my story not be about my characters? That's ridiculous.

Is it?

In George Axelrod and Billy Wilder's *The Seven Year Itch*, Marilyn Monroe's character doesn't even have a name. She's "the girl." The Curious George children's book series has a supporting character called "the man with the yellow hat." He has no name. We know him because he's the man with the yellow hat. The novel *Of Mice and Men* refers to Curly's wife as, you guessed it: "Curly's wife." This is not because these characters are not vital to the story; it's because they are vehicles through which we deliver our story, like the Sorting Hat in the Harry Potter series.

What am I supposed to write my story with if it's not about words? Marbles? Should I gather one thousand puppies in an arena, dress them up in different sweaters, and say, "Here's my story!"

What's in a word?

The answer: not much.

One standout quality of many unskilled storytellers is they overcomplicate their stories, throwing in "everything but the kitchen sink," as the editorial cliché goes. Another mark of an amateur storyteller is overwriting in general. First-time writers sometimes think: *the bigger the words, the denser the imagery, the longer the book, the smarter I'll sound.* They end up overwriting by up to fifty percent.

It's not about the words; it's about how your story impacts your reader. If your goal is to create a commercially successful story, this should become your mantra.

Of course, your choice of words and style are extremely important to your storytelling career, But, some of the wealthiest storytellers, like James Patterson, Danielle Steel, and Stephenie Meyers aren't exactly considered wordsmiths. They know that, whether a story is a novel or a film, it depends more on *images* than on *words*. The same story can be retold using entirely different words because story is the *shape* beneath the words, not the words themselves. The Pet Fish joke can be told using catfish instead of sac-a-lait, the antagonist a sheriff instead of a game warden, the protagonist a redneck instead of a Cajun, etc.

It's not the words that make meaning in the audience's minds; it's the emotions and actions beneath or beyond the words. You can say "I love you" just as effectively using the words, "You know how much I hate you, don't you?" if "I love you" is the emotion.

Okay, so it's not about you, and it's not about your characters, and it's not about the words.

What *is* it about?

The All-Important Reader

Without a reader or audience, a commercial story simply does not exist. Yes, you can sit in a corner, in a cave, on a riverbank, in a math class, or on a front porch telling stories. But no one is going to pay you when you do that.

Plus, I dare you to sit on your front steps and tell a story with *no audience*. That exercise will show you how important the audience is to the storyteller.

And the money (and satisfaction) comes when you tell a story to a reader or an audience. The millions come only when you tell your story to the world.

Knowing the audience's expectations and knowing how to play them is essential to telling a great story. If you master the psychology of your audience, as Boz Luhrmann or Stephen King or Ridley Scott or Alfred Hitchcock or William Goldman have done repeatedly, you're on your way to commercial success.

The guiding psychology is *not* the psychology of the storyteller—*your* psychology is of little interest to the audience. Let's be clear on that: No one really cares that you're devastated by your spouse's behavior. It's not about you. Nor is it about the psychology of your fictional characters, though a little bit of their psychology may be important in structuring the mechanism of your novel. Commercial storytelling isn't about your characters.

Instead, commercial storytelling is knowing your audience's expectations and knowing how to play them. That's what makes a writer like Stephen King or directors like Ridley Scott or Alfred Hitchcock or Christopher Nolan or James Cameron master storytellers. When an audience relates to a story, they relate to all its characters, as well as to the big picture. It doesn't matter if the story itself doesn't resemble their lives. If you feel elated when you leave the theater after a horror film, it's because you've allowed the monsters to be discharged and contained (or tamed) by the drama. After seeing *Alien* or *Oldboy*, your struggles at the office seem almost trivial: "I thought *I* had problems!" If, during the credits of *Gone Girl*, you turn to your girlfriend and say, "Wow, that movie made my marriage look like an episode of *Friends*," the psychological thriller was a success. It met your expectations, and you leave the theater feeling elated, satisfied, satiated…and damned lucky, too.

Suspension of Disbelief

Suspension of disbelief is an essential element of the psychology of the audience. Every reader begins a book prepared to suspend her disbelief and to allow the story to work its magic on her. That's the reader's gift to the story and to the storyteller. As long as the story doesn't fail her, the reader continues turning the pages; the moviegoer remains seated.

But the minute a story demands too much suspension of disbelief, stretches the reader's credence, the reader begins to lose trust in the storyteller. If that demand continues, the book will close, the remote control will do its nasty channel dance, and the reader will move on to a storyteller who understands the art of *suspended disbelief.*

*Veteran storytellers know they're allowed "one **gimme**."* The gimme in Alfred Hitchcock's *The Birds* is that birds have become a single-minded army of vicious killers and nothing can stop them. If Hitchcock had also given them opposable thumbs and the ability to drive a stick shift, the movie would not have been a hit. But Hitchcock only asked that you suspend your belief by imagining they are vicious killers that are all working together, and so you, the audience, are willing to exchange logic for thrill in that one regard.

One of my all-time favorite novels, William Wharton's *Birdy,* takes us from the protagonist's adolescence to his young adulthood to the Vietnam War to an Army sanatorium. The story moves back and forth freely in time based on a *single* dramatic gimme: the protagonist believes he is a bird. His post-war shell shock is revealed when attendants find him perched naked on his bedpost.

In *Birdman,* the audience believes, as with movies like *Superman,* *Batman,* *Spiderman,* and *Antman,* that Riggan Thomas a.k.a. "Birdman," is more than just a man, and can therefore overcome things regular people can't. They want to escape into the possibility of being more than just human themselves and overcome the impossible, and so they buy into this notion and partake in Birdman's journey.

In one of Lisa's favorite books, *Life of Pi* by Yann Martel, the gimme is we are supposed to believe in the possibility that a boy could survive on a boat lost at sea for months with a Bengal tiger. By book's end, we understand this is more than a boat ride with the unlikeliest of passengers. We are left to ponder: Was that real? An **allegory**? But

63

no matter how we feel by book's end, our one gimme got us there satisfactorily; we turned page after page in anticipation—to see what Pi would do next to survive one more day with the Bengal tiger he named Richard Parker.

Great Stories Appeal to Our Inner Child

Consider that every reader/audience member moves between two states of interaction with a story: that of the child, and that of the critic. The child, eager to be entertained, easily suspends his disbelief and holds onto that suspension against all odds—giving the story more than one chance to satisfy him or let him down. His relationship to the story is primarily emotional. The critic, by contrast, *never* completely suspends his disbelief. He remains detached from the story as he watches it so that he can logically find fault with it, thereby proving his own superior intelligence.

If you're lucky enough to be "the child," you've experienced how uncomfortable it can be watching a film in the company of "the critic." While you are lost in the story, the critic is ever ready to find fault, squinting at the dialogue to make sure it makes sense, poking you in the ribs when he spots a continuity problem ("That lamppost was closer to the actor in the previous shot!"), and in general, doesn't allow himself—or you—to be carried away or lost in the story.

From the opening strains of the popcorn and drinks commercial, the child viewer is immediately transported into whatever world is about to be revealed on the screen. The child *wants* to be swept away, lost in the story. He *wants* to be entertained or edified. When the child leaves the theater, he cringes to hear the critic immediately begin tearing the film apart. The child may be able to play the critic, too, but prefers to remain in the spell of the film for a little while at least.

("Could we just wait until we get to the bar before you start?" she begs the critic.)

Storytellers who know what they're doing focus on pleasing the children in the audience, knowing that the critics will have their say no matter what. If they can hold the child in that state of being, they're home free— satisfying the child's expectations. But if the film fails to tell its story compellingly, the child may turn critic in a heartbeat, his suspension of disbelief shattered by having to swallow so many "gimmes" that the spell of the story is broken for him.

When an editor says your book has "everything in it but the kitchen sink," he's saying you've delivered too many elements for the child to swallow and have defeated his ability to be lost in the story. (Keep in mind, the elements aren't limited only to gimmes. Overwriting refers to anything on your page that is not necessary to tell your story.)

H.P. Mallory became a direct-published paranormal e-novelist. Her first book sold 70,000 copies in less than six months. Her success caught the attention of the traditional publisher behind bestselling authors like Danielle Steele, George R.R. Martin, Dean Koontz, Janet Evanovich, Stephen Hawking, and others. She signed a three-book contract with Random House. "Selling e-books on Kindle and Barnesandnoble.com basically changed my life," Mallory says. "I never would have gotten where I am today if I hadn't."

5

SECONDARY STORY ELEMENTS

IN ADDITION TO THE FIVE primary story elements we examined in Chapter 3 (Character, Conflict, Scene, Structure, and Theme/Premise), the professional storyteller needs to master a few important secondary elements:

1. Setting
2. **Point of View**
3. **Tone of Voice** (narration)
4. Dialogue
5. Dialogue Tags
6. Summary
7. Prologue
8. Tunneling
9. **Epilogue**

1—*Setting*

In the best stories, setting is almost as important as the primary story elements: *Revenant, Dunkirk, Passengers, Alien, The Martian.* Consider James Cameron's *Titanic* without the ship, John Carpenter's *The Thing* without Antarctica, or Tate Taylor's *The Help* without Mississippi. But instead of exhaustively researching setting during your first draft, write it first from your imagination. Describe your setting as you remember or imagine places and you'll present the most vivid aspects of them, which will make your story more dramatic. Don't confuse your vision by doing research prematurely. If you need to double-check your facts, do that only during revision. This lets you paint the setting from your heart.

Here's an old writer's trick: If your story fits together pretty well, but lacks energy, to make it come alive consider *changing the setting* to somewhere more dramatic.

2—*Point of View*

Point of view is that intangible element of narrative that defines the storyteller's relationship to his story and to his audience. It's often confused with tone of voice, which we'll discuss next. The point of view is embodied, in your story, in the character of the narrator, who may be more or less visible to the reader. Ishmael in Melville's *Moby-Dick* is a *visible* narrator: "Call me Ishmael," the novel's opening words, establishes him as the storyteller the reader learns to trust. The narrator in Leo Tolstoy's *War and Peace* is invisible, and "omniscient"—he knows everything that's happening both inside and outside his characters. Storytellers have used many points of view to aid them in telling their stories effectively, though the best storytellers almost always choose a single point of view per story.

Personal point of view, usually in the form of **first-person narrative,** is when the storyteller places the narrator into the story—so that the reader experiences the story through the eyes of this character. Most of the time, we align ourselves with this narrator, rooting for him every step of the way, from Holden Caulfield to Scout to Bridget Jones to Katniss. In William Shakespeare's *Richard III,* however, the protagonist introduces himself to the audience in a **monologue** that wins us over to an extremely unsympathetic narrator-protagonist. This is the epitome of the term sympathetic—a character we *suffer with.*

With POV, it's important to understand we don't have to love the narrator; we must believe him and believe that he believes in himself. Chuck Palahniuk, Author of *Fight Club,* is famous for using extreme characters to narrate his stories. In a later work, *Choke,* Palahniuk creates protagonist Victor Mancini—a thirty-something-year-old guy who's a med-school dropout, goes to sex addicts' anonymous groups to get laid, and chokes in upscale restaurants as a way of making extra money to not only pay for his mom's medical expenses but elicit affection from strangers. Do we like this guy? No. Do we believe in his strength and authenticity as a character and narrator? We do. Even in the opening of *Choke,* Victor Mancini tells us we're not going to like him or his story:

> What happens here is first going to piss you off. After that, it just gets worse and worse. What you're getting here is a stupid true-life story about nobody you'd ever want to meet.

This is, in fact, what we get, except we want to read it. We're engaged. The author hooked us, and so we read on. Chuck

Palahniuk's narrative point of view is so strong in all his works that his style has been said to be a genre of its own.

Third-person close or **third-person limited**, is when the narrator stands outside the story to tell it, but from the perspective of the main character. This means we know what this one character is thinking and feeling, but we can only interpret how other characters may think or feel by way of observation (through this main character). When writing a story using third-person close narration, you must be careful not to head hop.

The Giver by Lois Lowry

> Now, thinking about the feeling of fear as he pedaled home along the river path, he remembered that moment of palpable, stomach-sinking terror when the aircraft had streaked above. It was not what he was feeling with December approaching. He searched for the right word to describe his own feeling.
>
> Jonas was careful about language. Not like his friend, Asher, who talked too fast and mixed things up, scrambling words and phrases until they were barely recognizable and often very funny.

From this third-person close narrative POV, we know what Jonas is thinking and feeling (terror), but we only know what the other characters may think or feel from Jonas's perspective. Asher talks too fast and mixes things up because Jonas has witnessed this. If Jonas had never witnessed this, we (the reader) would not be aware of Asher's trait.

Another point of view prevalent in classic literature is **third-person omniscient**, where the narrator knows everything inside and outside the story's characters and makes the reader privy to the way every character thinks and feels and provides glimpses of the past and future to put present events in context. It's a wonderful way to present a story from every perspective, but when starting out, it can be confusing—being inside everyone's head—and it can weigh down the pace.

> Many years later, as he faced the firing squad, Colonel Aureliano Buendia was to remember that distant afternoon when his father took him to discover ice. At that time Macondo was a village of twenty adobe houses, built on the bank of a river of clear water that ran along a bed of polished stones, which were white and enormous, like prehistoric eggs. The world was so recent that many things lacked names, and in order to indicate them it was necessary to point…

The opening lines of Gabriel García Márquez's *One Hundred Years of Solitude* establishes his narrator as omniscient, omnipresent, omnipotent—the God who creates a fictional world as he speaks it. The reader is swept along into his **magical realism** by the narrator's voice. Keep in mind the omniscient POV doesn't have to be narrated by God or a god, or by an all-knowing spirit or Death—in the case of *The Book Thief* by Markus Zusak—a writer can tell her story through the eyes of every character. Here's a great example:

Everything I Never Told You by Celeste Ng

> Marilyn closes her eyes. Maybe, when she opens them, Lydia will be there, covers pulled over her head as usual, wisps of hair trailing from beneath. A grumpy lump bundled

under the bedspread that she'd somehow missed before. I was in the bathroom, Mom. I went downstairs for some water. I was lying right here all the time. Of course, when she looks, nothing has changed. The closed curtains glow like a blank television screen.

Downstairs, she stops in the doorway of the kitchen, a hand on each side of the frame. Her silence says everything. "I'll check outside," she says at last. "Maybe for some reason…" She keeps her gaze trained on the floor as she heads for the front door, as if Lydia's footprints might be crushed into the hall runner.

Nath says to Hannah, "She was in her room last night. I heard her radio playing. At eleven thirty." He stops, remembering that he had not said goodnight.

We go from Marilyn to Nath's head. The narration flows. We understand from the opening of the book, we're going to be "a fly on the wall"—in the mind of every character in the book. For more on point of view, read Sandra Gerth's *Point of View: How to Use the Different Point of View Types, Avoid Head-hopping, and Choose the Best Point of View for Your Book;* or Mary Kennedy's *Point of View.*

3—*Tone of Voice*

Tone of voice is simply the attitude behind the narrator's point of view, which is not to be confused with the author's POV. Tone assists in telling a story more effectively. Tone adds specificity and lends emotional credibility to how the material is presented, affecting how the reader processes the story. When Uncle Wib was telling a ghost story, his voice would hush so that we on the porch had to strain forward to listen and not miss a word. "It was a cold and windy night, and the trees were so frightened their limbs didn't dare move." That tone of voice was very different from that used in telling a hunting yarn where the storyteller's awareness of preposterous exaggeration was clear in his **diction**—his choice of words. The storyteller's tone of voice in a horror story is going to be quite different from that in a comedy or a fairy tale.

> When the little boy next faced the mirror, his heart stopped. A second ago, a girl he'd never seen before had been facing him. This time, not even his own face looked back. He screamed and ran away.

Tone of voice, then, is created through diction, **syntax,** and point of view.

Here are two examples of stories with distinct but very different tones of voice—narrated by young male leads.

The Outsiders by S. E. Hinton

> Soda is handsomer than anyone else I know. Not like Darry—Soda's movie-star kind of handsome, the kind that people stop on the street to watch go by. He's not as tall as Darry, and he's a little slimmer, but he has a finely drawn, sensitive face that somehow manages to be reckless and thoughtful at the same time. He's got dark-gold hair that he combs back—long and silky and straight—and in the summer the sun bleaches it to a shining wheat gold. His eyes are dark brown—lively, dancing, recklessly laughing eyes that can be gentle and sympathetic one moment and blazing with anger the next. He has Dad's eyes, but Soda is one of a kind. He can get drunk in a drag race or dancing

without ever getting near alcohol. In our neighborhood it's rare to find a kid who doesn't drink once in a while. But Soda never touches a drop—he doesn't need to. He gets drunk on just plain living. And he understands everybody.

High Fidelity by Nick Hornby

My desert-island, all-time, top five most memorable split-ups, in chronological order:

1. Alison Ashworth
2. Penny Hardwick
3. Jackie Allen
4. Charlie Nicholson
5. Sarah Kendrew

Can you see your name in that lot, Laura? I reckon you'd sneak into the top ten, but there's no place for you in the top five; those places are reserved for the kind of humiliations and heartbreaks that you're just not capable of delivering. That probably sounds crueler than it is meant to, but the fact is that we're too old to make each other miserable, and that's a good thing, not a bad thing, so don't take your failure to make the list personally. Those days are gone, and a good fucking riddance to them; unhappiness really meant something back then. Now it's a drag, like a cold or having no money. If you really wanted to mess me up, you should have gotten to me earlier.

Ponyboy is a poor, parent-less young teen, while Rob is older, middle class, more educated. Technically, you might think the diction in *High Fidelity* would be more sophisticated, and maybe if we broke down each word individually it would be, but because of the big difference in syntax, *The Outsiders* is rich with imagery and figurative language. The narration is elegant and subdued, not how you imagine a poor gang member from the wrong side of the tracks to talk. It changes, deepens, the impact of the story; we know the story Ponyboy is about to tell is going to break our hearts. The narrative tone in *High Fidelity* is angry, cynical, wry, as record store owner Rob's point of view is that of a man that's been wounded one too many times by love; it's edgier than *The Outsiders*, even though the setting and circumstances are not.

Note that the diction of Melville's *Moby-Dick* is serious and solemn, what we would call "mythic." The mythic diction of García Márquez's opening is enhanced by a playful undertone shown in word-choice and word-placement ("to discover ice," "like prehistoric eggs"). Sometimes, in editing a story, and depending on its nature, we simply replace prosaic words with mythic words more in keeping with creating the intended effect on the audience.

4—Dialogue

Two kinds of action drive your story forward, compelling the reader along with it: *action proper* and *dialogue*.

Action proper is easy to understand, and therefore to master. It's the kicks, the gunfire, the crashes, the falls from roofs that rivet the audience to "what happens next":

- She opened the front door to find him facing her with a gun.
- He withdrew, rolled over, and left the bed without a word.
- The missile struck the center of the complex, obliterating it, the six terrorists, and every woman and child with them.

The second kind of action, which is dialogue, is more difficult for inexperienced writers because it's often confused with the speech of everyday life. Dramatic dialogue, just as much as action proper, must move the story forward. There's no room in your story for "hellos" and "goodbyes," for "how's the weather?" or "how's it going?" Dialogue is not conversation. Dialogue *holds* attention; conversation causes folks to reach for their remotes.

Here's a section of dialogue from a novel that serves the story more effectively than description would. It engages us, sets the tone, and propels the action/motivation for the entire story forward—particularly the last line in this section.

William Golding's *Lord of the Flies*

> Piggy persisted. "This is an island, isn't it?"
>
> "I climbed a rock," said Ralph slowly, "and I think this is an island."
>
> "They're all dead," said Piggy, "'an' this is an island. Nobody knows we're here. Your dad don't know. Nobody knows—" His lips quivered and the spectacles dimmed with mist.
>
> "We may stay here till we die."

Here are some examples of memorable movie lines (dialogue) that propels the action forward:

1. You're going to need a bigger boat. (*Jaws*)
2. I love the smell of napalm in the morning. (*Apocalypse Now*)
3. I'm having an old friend for dinner. (*Silence of the Lambs*)

4. I don't care if you're half monkey or half ape, I'm getting you out of here. (*Boys Don't Cry*)
5. I have to go see about a girl. (*Good Will Hunting*)
6. Shut up. Just shut up. You had me at hello. (*Jerry Maguire*)
7. Am I an island? I am bloody Ibiza! (*About a Boy*)
8. Hey, don't get hit by a bus. Or do. Whatever. (*What Happens in Vegas*)
9. I'm the backup parent. The understudy. (*The Descendants*)

ER ORDERLY
Are you suffering from something?

KAY
Just writer's block.

(*Stranger than Fiction*)

5—Dialogue Tags

While dialogue is a powerful vehicle with which to convey your story's progress, **dialogue tags** can be the kiss of death. The tag is the words following a piece of dialogue like "he quipped," "she chirped," "he guffawed." Stick to "said," if you must, rather than using such comic book verbs. If you remember only one thing, remember this: the sole purpose of a dialogue tag is clarification. An effective writer needn't have to tell us their character is screaming, crying, gasping, moving, turning, nodding, blinking, shaking his head, furrowing her brow, cocking his head, rolling her eyes, clearing his throat, putting her hands on her hips, gazing into his lover's eyes, looking at, looking away, looking up, looking down, raising his voice, lowering her voice, whispering, or saying something: coyly, cutely, angrily, happily, cynically, sarcastically, joyfully, sincerely, insincerely, while smiling, while grimacing—you get the gist. Tags like this aren't any less exhausting when you spread them throughout your novel; trust us on this one. Using dialogue tags for clarification *only* tells your readers that you're confident in your execution and trust they will interpret your story correctly. Review Ernest Hemingway's short stories to understand the power that comes from keeping it simple: "Would you please please please please please please stop talking?"

6—*Summary*

Scenes, which we've discussed in the last chapter, take place in real time, right in front of the audience's or reader's eyes. Nothing is hidden, action fully apparent—*showing*, not *telling*. **Summary** tells the reader or audience what happened in the **background** of the story that explains the scene we just saw or the one to come. Summary clarifies or details plot points to give the reader information he needs to understand the story. When you hear an editor say, "Show, don't tell," it's because you've summarized a part of your story that would be more effectively written as a scene—because the scene *shows* the reader the action. New writers often avoid drama because it's much more challenging to write, exchanging it for the easier summary approach, thereby disappointing readers who want to *see action happen,* who want to *witness the drama.*

But there's a place for summary in every story. It can be more effective in setting a mood in some instances. A master of commercial fiction uses summary to introduce his second main character, the antagonist.

Here's a scene from Stephen King's *Fire-Starter* (Horror):

At the moment Cap Hollister had his passing thought about him, John Rainbird was sitting in his room at the Mayflower Hotel watching a television game called *The Crosswits*. He was naked. He sat in the chair with his bare feet neatly together and watched the program. He was waiting for it to get dark. After it got dark, he would begin waiting for it to get late. When it was late, he would begin waiting for it to get early. When it got early, he would stop waiting and go upstairs to Room 1217 and kill Dr. Wanless. Then he would come down here and think about whatever Wanless would have told him before he died, and sometime after the sun came up, he would sleep briefly.

John Rainbird was a man at peace. He was at peace with almost everything—Cap, the Shop, the United States. He was at peace with God, Satan, and the universe. If he was not yet at complete peace with himself, that was only because his pilgrimage was not yet over. He had many coups, many honorable scars. It did not matter that people turned away from him in fear and loathing. It did not matter that he had lost one eye in Vietnam. What they paid him did not matter. He took it and most of it went to buy shoes. He had a great love of shoes. He owned a home in Flagstaff, and although he rarely went there himself, he had all his shoes sent there. When he did get a chance to go to his house, he admired the shoes—Gucci, Bally, Bass, Adidas, Van Donen. Shoes. His house was a strange forest: shoe trees grew in every room, and he would go from room to room admiring the shoefruit that grew on them. But when he was alone, he went barefoot. His father, a full-blooded Cherokee, had been buried barefoot. Someone had stolen his burial moccasins.

Other than shoes, John Rainbird was interested in only two things. One of them was death. His own death, of course; he had been preparing for this inevitability for twenty years or more. Dealing death had always been his business and was the only trade he had ever excelled at. He became more and more interested in it as he grew older, as an artist will become more interested in the qualities and levels of light, as writers will feel for character and nuance like blind men reading braille. What interested him most was the actual leaving...the actual exhalation of the soul...the exit from the body and what human beings knew as life and the passing into something else. What must it be like to feel yourself slipping away? Did you think it was a dream from which you would awake? Was the Christian devil there with his fork, ready to jam it through your shrieking soul and carry it down to hell like a piece of meat on a shish kebab? Was there joy? Did you know you were going? What is it that the eyes of the dying see?

Rainbird hoped he would have the opportunity to find out for himself. In his business, death was often quick and unexpected, something that happened in the flick of an eye. He hoped that when his own death came, he would have time to prepare and feel everything. More and more lately he had watched the faces of the people he killed, trying to see the secret in the eyes.

Death interested him.

What also interested him was the little girl they were so concerned with. This Charlene McGee. As far as Cap knew, John Rainbird had only the vaguest knowledge of the

McGees and none at all of Lot Six. Actually, Rainbird knew almost as much as Cap himself—something that surely would have marked him for extreme sanction if Cap had known. They suspected that the girl had some great or potentially great power—maybe a whole batch of them. He would like to meet this girl and see what her powers were. He also knew that any McGee was what Cap called "a potential mental dominant," but that did not concern John Rainbird. He had not yet met a man who could dominate him.

The Crosswits ended. The news came on. None of it was good. John Rainbird sat, not eating, not drinking, not smoking, clean and empty and husked out, and waited for the killing time to come around.

This singular scene is orchestrated like a concerto, with a compelling hook—the naked man on the bed of a famous DC luxury hotel watching a humdrum television show. How can we not continue reading? We're compelled to find out what he's doing, and why he's naked. When we then learn that he's a killer waiting for his kill, we're fully hooked and want to know more. Stephen King creates the same kind of anticipation as C. S. Lewis did using a string of action scenes in *The Lion, the Witch and the Wardrobe*, only King creates the anxiety in our guts using summary—without his character moving from his spot on the bed or so much as twitching. He foreshadows effectively by telling us what the antagonist is waiting for—to kill a man. And then, during the waiting, he takes us into the mind, *and heart*, of our killer. What Stephen King does here is use summary within a single scene to hook the reader and move the story. He engages us with this technique. Do we wish he would have written a scene where we see this killer out shopping for shoes? No, that would be a waste of words and action, and it would stray from the story. In this case, summary is the most effective way to go, as it brings clarity to the details we need to understand the antagonist. He loves shoes because he was damaged irreversibly when his father's shoes were stolen from his dead body. The childhood trauma strengthens Rainbird and provides his motivation.

7—Prologue

A **prologue** is the opening section of a work of fiction that hooks the reader or sets the stage with provocative background information or that highlights the stakes of the story about to begin. Sometimes a prologue relays background details crucial to understanding the story, and that usually takes place in the past. Sometimes the prologue presents an exciting action scene that might occur anywhere at all in the story. Prologues aren't *necessary* to every story, and some readers say they don't even bother to read prologues. Without a prologue, the information or drama it provides must simply find a way to tunnel itself into the story as it moves forward. But only the ringmaster— you!—can decide whether to use prologue or tunneling. Author Elmore Leonard's second rule in his 10 Rules for Writing is: Avoid prologues. "They can be annoying. A prologue in a novel is backstory, and you can drop it in anywhere you want."

Think about whether having a prologue is worth it. If it is, go for it.

You want to read a prologue that does its job? Google: "*Jurassic Park* the Prologue" by Michael Crichton. While this passage would interrupt flow if placed almost anywhere in the book, at its opening it sets the tone and serves as a warning. Here's the final paragraph in the Prologue:

...A hundred years ago we didn't have cars, airplanes, computers or vaccines. It was a whole different world, but to the earth, a hundred years is nothing. A million years is nothing. This planet lives and breathes on a much vaster scale. We can't imagine its slow and powerful rhythms, and we haven't got the humility to try. We've been residents here for the blink of an eye. If we're gone tomorrow, the earth will not miss us.

8—*Tunneling*

An effective device for getting vital details into a story without boring the reader by making him read five, ten, twenty, fifty or more pages that set up the story, is tunneling. A storyteller can start the action on page one, and then tunnel in any important details that are necessary for the story, but that would not be as exciting as a scene or would not work as effectively if the story started further back in time.

The Secret Life of Bees by Sue Monk Kidd opens with the book's fourteen-year-old lead in bed on a hot summer night in 1964. She's waiting for the bees to come so their collective buzz can lull her to sleep. Because the story is told in the first person, there's easy and ample opportunity to tunnel, as we are carried through this journey from the protagonist's perspective, from inside her head.

On page four, close to midnight, Lily Owens finally hears the hum of the bees. But this night, they don't stay outside her window. They break in and form a cloud-like swarm in the middle of her bedroom. She runs and grabs her father, a man she calls T. Ray, who admonishes her for waking him up and acting crazy. Lily returns to bed. The next paragraph begins with the line: "My first and only memory of my mother was the day she died." And Lily takes us through that day, December 3, 1954, some ten years earlier, play by play, ending with:

> When I saw the gun in her hand, I ran toward her, clumsy and falling, wanting to save her, wanting to save us all.
>
> Time folded in on itself then. What is left lies in clear disjointed pieces in my head. The gun shining like a toy in her hand, how he snatched it away and waved it around. The gun on the floor. Bending to pick it up. The noise that exploded around us.
>
> This is what I know about myself. She was all I wanted. And I took her away.

The paragraph that follows (after the double space to denote the transition), takes us back to present day, where Lily proceeds to describe what the farm looks like where she and T. Ray reside.

Would this story be as effective had it started on that horrific day ten years earlier? No. For starters, we'd have a four-year-old narrator, as opposed to fourteen. Lily's awakening, journey, and healing occur because of the bees, and because she's at an age, and time, in her young life when she's ready to face the thing that's haunted her for the last decade—the accidental death of her mom. Using traditional chronology (arranging the events revealed in a story in order of their occurrence) wouldn't serve this story, as words and pages would be wasted on telling things that "are not this story." The day Lily started kindergarten is not relevant to this story, nor is losing her first tooth, or learning to ride a bike. Tunneling is a wonderful tool to assist in telling your story—it creates dramatic flow, meaning events are delivered to the reader in a way that maintains pace and builds suspense, not necessarily in the order they occurred. Tunneling can also help you remove everything that is not your story. Take a look at any set-up or backstory you have in a manuscript you're currently working on (if you have one), and reread it with these new eyes, asking yourself if you need everything. Our guess is you don't. Pluck the part you need from the rest and save it in a separate Word document. Then, when you do another draft, use your instincts to see where this information could be tunneled in to best serve your story while keeping the reader engaged and without interrupting the pace.

9—*Epilogue*

An epilogue goes at the end of your story and is used by the storyteller to tie up any loose ends regarding plot or character that the reader may need to feel fully satisfied with your story. In some cases, the epilogue may serve to entice readers to look for the "next installment" in your series. Tying up the fate of every character and all loose ends isn't necessary to ensure every reader's satisfaction and can even seem indulgent or revealing of the storyteller's lack of self-confidence. That's why epilogues are as optional as prologues.

Sometimes you need to rely on instinct followed by a professional opinion (from your editor) when deciding if an epilogue is necessary. One thing that's important to note is that no two readers (or audience members) are going to react the same way to your story. Oftentimes in the case of romances, when the two leads finally get together at the end (or don't), there's a certain degree of intentional ambiguity— a loose end.

I have to go see about a girl, Will Hunting writes in his farewell note to Sean Maguire. We are left with a sense of hope. We're inspired. But, do we feel one hundred percent secure that "the girl he's going to see about" will welcome him with open arms? If you're a romantic like Lisa, you sat in your theatre seat after seeing *Good Will Hunting* for the first time and—after bathing in the sweet satisfaction of a story well told—you "wrote" the epilogue in your head. Will gets to LA Knocks on Skylar's door. She opens it, pauses, and then falls into his arms. Maybe you fast forwarded right to their wedding day, to their first child, to Will working for NASA and the happily ever after.

If this Academy Award winner were a book, do you think it would benefit from an epilogue? In this case, no. The ending was hopeful enough. Inspiring enough. It wrapped things up with Will "enough." We believe in his growth and trust in his future. And that's all we wanted to be reassured of, that *good* Will Hunting is going to be okay. This story did its job.

> "Know what the best part of my day is?" [Will's best friend Chuckie asks him.] "The ten seconds from when I pull up to the curb till when I get to your door. 'Cause I think maybe I'll get up there and I'll knock on your door, and you won't be there. No goodbye, no see ya later, no nothing. You just left. I don't know much, but I know that."

The ending to *Good Will Hunting* satisfies Chuckie's, and our, greatest hope for Will.

Rather than list books with great epilogues, it may be more beneficial to consider the books that had endings that frustrated you or made you (want to) toss them out the window. You spent, after all, five, ten, twenty hours of your life invested in their story—and for what?! Those are hours you'll never get back. You could've been exercising, sleeping, remodeling the kitchen, or writing your own great story.

The *New York Times* bestseller-turned-series, *The Handmaid's Tale* by Margaret Atwood has one such open-ended ending. One might argue it's frustrating because it's dismal. Others call it unfinished, yet true to life. "True to life" is what we've been preaching against. There is no ending in real life, except the one most of us fear. Is that the feeling Atwood intended to leave the reader with—one of fear and frustration? It's been called anti-climactic—a swear word in the world of storytelling. Is that the emotion she was going for? If so, the ending's a big success.

Know that being satisfied by an ending doesn't equate with it being a happy one. We are satisfied by the ending of *Romeo & Juliet*, but not happy two teenagers in love are now dead. Similarly, we are relieved by the ending of *The English Patient*, but not happy—just relieved the lead's physical and emotional suffering has come to a (compassionate) end. So, what's frustrating then, and where an epilogue might come in handy, is when we read the last sentence in a book, but then turn the page looking for another chapter, or…the epilogue.

These are all the things you want to consider before creating prologues and epilogues.

6

DO I NEED EDITORIAL HELP?

"The story is always better than your ability to write it."

—Robin McKinley
Winner of the Newberry Medal for *The Hero and the Crown*

YES, YOU DO.

Even if you're an experienced writer, your work needs an objective eye before it goes before the public. An objective eye, by definition, does not belong to your spouse, partner, best friend, family member, or friend. Their role is to support you, not criticize you. Unless you want to join the growing percentage of all books published that are badly written and unprofessional, and therefore clog the arteries of the internet with mediocrity, submit your story to a professional who can help you polish it to perfection.

There are several levels or kinds of editing: conceptual editing, structural editing, style editing, and copyediting.

Let's examine them in their most effective chronological order.

Conceptual/Developmental Editing

Conceptual editing focuses on the story's overall concept, in terms of both marketability and genre. Does it address the needs of an identifiable market? Does it fit into an identifiable genre like "sci-fi thriller," "romance novel," or "mystery"? Does it contain the necessary components for that genre?

A good conceptual editor helps prevent your novel from being what the story merchants call "a feathered fish"—that is, a book or screenplay that prospective buyers don't quite know how to define. This editor helps you rework your story beyond its structure. This includes removing everything you have in there that isn't your story—what Richard Lanham terms "the **Lard Factor.**" This can be, as we mentioned earlier, up to half your book. It's a conceptual editor's job to assist in turning your project into one solid story that is focused and coherent.

Equally important, a good conceptual editor helps you remove elements that mitigate the marketability of your book and enhance elements that make it more marketable. Is the protagonist of your mainstream romance only fifteen? Make her seventeen or eighteen! Is your antagonist the president of the United States? Does he have to be?

Structural Editing

Once the concept of your story is refined, the structural editor guides you through the **obligatory** components of the *kind of story* you're hoping to publish or get produced. Do these components appear in their most dramatic order? If it's a romantic comedy, the two lovers "meet cute," fall in love, run into obstacles, then resolve the obstacles and end up together. A storyteller's job is to make these simple, obligatory elements appear fresh and original; it's not to replace them with something "original," which would disappoint the enormous audience who loves romantic comedies. The structural editor will make sure the story proceeds from beginning to middle to end in maximum dramatic order. Does your story start on page one? You can be sure of it if you hire a fantastic structural editor. The structural editor can teach you valuable writing tips to make each sentence count in your story and teach you how to restructure your sentences so that you remove extraneous words and phrases, repetitive words, or excessive dialogue tags from your story. This brings us to—

Style Editing

Your style must serve your story, instead of getting in its way. The style editor, readdressing the Lard Factor, removes unnecessary words, especially adverbs and adjectives; academic or Latinate words like "however," "moreover," "thus," "therefore," "thereby," "very," that impede your reader's easy progress through your story; inconsistencies of tense; inaccuracies of grammar and syntax; and redundancies of sentence structure. In general, the style editor makes your story as readable as can be. Writers in love with their own words are not great storytellers. The great storyteller gets out of the way of his story. Remember that Aristotle noted that in the stories of Homer, the author himself was nowhere; his characters, everywhere.

The style editor also makes your diction consistent, making sure a character that's a professor speaks like a professor, while one that's a bus driver speaks like a bus driver. The editor also makes sure that your story's tone of voice is clear by pointing out diction that makes it inconsistent or confusing. Every writer wishing to improve her style needs to read, and reread, *The Elements of Style* by William Strunk, Jr.

It's exciting to see the results of a solid structural and/or style edit. Sometimes two, three, even five thousand words can be removed from a story without cutting down on the number of sentences. Imagine the kind of improvement on pacing and flow this has on a story.

Copy Editing a.k.a. Line Editing

The final stage of the editorial process is copy editing, in which the editor corrects spelling and punctuation mistakes, checks every fact in your story and/or points them out for you to fact check, and makes sure that your "usage"—things like capitalization of titles, the spelling out of numbers, and paragraphing—are both accurate and consistent. Do not confuse copy editing with proofreading. A manuscript that has been carefully copy edited is ready to submit to traditional publishers for consideration, but it's not ready for worldwide publication without being proofed. (The best way to proofread a book is with a printed out copy and pen in hand.)

Getting started is the hard part. But before long, you, too, will feel like the book just wrote itself. We will help you get from where you are now to where you ought to be—in the company of professional storytellers, storytellers that are paid well to tell us stories we want to hear.

Today's world of commercial storytelling is a topsy-turvy new frontier, filled with new electronic delivery systems and traditional methods that are in imminent danger of extinction, or at least evolution. Yet such is our hunger for stories that new authors are still being discovered every minute, before our eyes.

Of the top 100 Kindle bestsellers that were published in 2016, traditional publishers held two-thirds of the market. Let's put this another way: Independent (Indie) publishers accounted for over thirty percent of e-books on Kindle's Top 100 list in 2016. Ten short years ago, KDP (Kindle Direct Publishing) was still being tested by beta users. Now, one-third of the top 100 bestsellers were written by authors who weren't signed by a traditional publisher.

If they can do it, why can't you?

Despite the vicissitudes in this modern-day story marketplace, almost nothing in today's world is more valuable than stories, or what the business world calls intellectual property.

We ask all our clients to allow us to be tough coaches to expedite the process by which their amateur status becomes professional. Whether a client stays with us or moves on, our pride in taking him or her from the front porch to the marketplace has made our life's work enormously satisfying.

For you, the stranger who hasn't worked with us one on one, this book distills what we've learned along the way. Our experience has generated numerous bestsellers and millions of dollars for the writers we've edited, coached, or managed.

Our goal with *Tell Your Story to the World and Sell It for Millions* is to inspire and instruct. We hope the success stories showcased so far have affected you at a deep level, all the way into the marrow of your writing bones. They've gotten into ours. We've seen storytellers become happy millionaires and fulfilled artists once they mastered the art of storytelling, and we want that for you.

What are you waiting for? Let's go for it!

From years of working with writers, we've discovered, in the drift toward a working methodology, that one good tool toward helping a writer in the middle of a dramatic project (novel, memoir, movie

treatment, screenplay, or stage play) is to recommend certain stories (and sometimes warn against others).

You don't know how to start your novel, but you know you want to write it in the first-person narrative. Your lead is a young underdog type, but you don't want him coming off pathetic, whiny, or like a victim. Here's a suggestion: Read *The Catcher in the Rye*, and do it like Salinger. Not "funny" enough for you? Try *Bridget Jones's Diary*. Not dramatic enough? Read *White Oleander* or *Wonder Woman* or *Hacksaw Ridge*. You want to write a feature that's all about comedic timing, but full of depth? Watch *Jerry Maguire* or *La La Land* with a pen and notebook in hand and jot down every scene as you go. You want to write a character piece, a real coming of age drama? Do the same thing with *Good Will Hunting* or *Moonlight*.

With a sound recommendation, your motivation and inspiration can be reinvigorated. At the end of the day, nothing teaches storytelling better than reading great stories.

Exercise 1

Right now, before you move on to Part II, The Business of Storytelling, *find a copy of your favorite novel and read it again, this time reading it as a craftsman would read it, not as a passive reader.* Let's look at the opening of *Dune* and notice little things that Frank Herbert did to create his desired effect:

> In the week before their departure to Arrakis, when all the final scurrying about had reached a nearly unbearable frenzy, an old crone came to visit the mother of the boy, Paul.

Note that Herbert's story begins *in medias res,* "in the middle of things," as Aristotle pointed out Homer's epics do. We are suddenly at the beginning of a scene—the story starts on page one—but the scene is deftly set up in time, its context, and the background activity: a busy place where many people move quickly to ready for departure. It's a momentous time, though we have no idea what "Arrakis" means. The air is filled with agitation that's "nearly unbearable." The protagonist of the scene, "an old crone," isn't named but given a description that troubles us. Only "Paul" is named, in a casual way of introducing the most important character of the thick novel we're holding in our hands.

> It was a warm night at Castle Caladan, and the ancient pile of stone that had served the Atreides family as home for twenty-six generations bore that cooled-sweat feeling it acquired before a change in the weather.

Never disappointing his reader, Herbert, our storyteller, takes the time to describe the *feeling* of the scene: "warm night," "cooled-sweat." While at the same time, he tunnels in more background information: the name of the castle, Paul's family name, their ancient lineage ("twenty-six generations") in this same residence, highlighting the importance of their departure. And the simple, metaphorical "change in the weather" further portends the massive historical change that's about to occur.

You can see, with this much parsing, that Herbert chose every word carefully here, as the scene goes on to build the suspense of who Paul Atreides is, where he and his family are going, and why he is so important to the world we're so quickly thrust into. In the same way, we broke down *The Lion, the Witch and the Wardrobe.* We looked at the opening like a craftsman would, breaking it down to a sequence of events that propelled us to our "middle" in six short pages.

Exercise 2

If you're really serious about learning the craft, outline your favorite novel or script, as long-time client Milli Meyer did. I will never forget the day she approached me after a seminar at UC/Riverside. "I'm not sure I understood everything," she began, shyly, "but I'm very excited about learning to write and I just need to know what you think of how I started." She then explained that she'd taken her favorite novel, John Steinbeck's *The Grapes of Wrath,* and *outlined it.* "I figured," she said, "if I could see the parts, I could build the whole." I congratulated Milli for being the most craftsmanlike person in the room. She was approaching the craft the way a carpenter would approach building his first table—by taking an existing table apart and observing how it fit together.

Do this with your favorite novel and the structure of how that story was built appears as if by magic. Except, now you see that it isn't magic that made this story great. It's first having a solid foundation, a solid structure. Now take that outline and number each sequence of events with one to ten dashes, according to the degree of conflict/resolution. Now turn your graph sideways to the left, and you can see the dramatic build throughout the book's middle.

What you will discover in doing this exercise is that there is a logical and practical way to build and tell a great story. And that's great news!

If your heart is set on your story becoming the next great feature or series for television, you can always study structure by downloading some of your favorite TV scripts here: https://sites.google.com/site/tvwriting.

Exercise 3

If you're too pressed for time and the exercise above sounds plain nuts, re-watch your favorite movie as a writer (not an audience member) and, with pen in hand, jot down each scene—and what it accomplishes:

- The opening scene happens on a subway. It introduces the protagonist, in action, and suggests that something is bothering her, something that bothers all of us.
- In Scene 2, on a busy street, the harshness of the environment is underlined in starkly dramatic strokes.
- Scene 3, at the office, introduces the antagonist and makes it clear that she is apparently remorseless and unstoppable, etc.

Once you've outlined the whole script, you see like a true craftsman "how the table is put together," and you can proceed to build your own with as many originalities as you can imagine while achieving an effective audience-moving structure.

Exercise 4

And if you're really a glutton for punishment, like most writers, go one step further: Type out the first twenty-five pages or so of your favorite novel or script. This will program your onboard computer—your muscle memory— to write well; making it *feel* wrong when you start writing less well.

Exercise 5

Read your favorite book out loud. (Yes, if you must, you can listen to it on audio—but listen like a writer!) This will prepare you for reading your own work out loud for the first time. This is Lisa's and many writers' final stage in the writing process, after a structural edit and before a copy edit. Will everyone be reading your book out loud? No, but if a book flows and tells the story it's meant to tell through oral narration, you can be sure it's going to be a hit with readers. And it's hard to let dialogue that *sounds* bad remain unedited.

"There's a misplaced, but widespread, idea that writing is easy."

After big success with an Amazon free giveaway of *The Black Mile*, **Mark Dawson** decided it was time to make money from all his labors. On his four-hour commute by train to and from work, he committed to writing a contemporary thriller series, publishing consistently using the "power of numbers" and Facebook as his main platform. The John Milton Series is nine books and counting since direct publishing book one, *The Cleaner,* in 2014.

PART II

"We're all in this together—a network of creative minds. Let's share in this abundant time. There's infinite space available for new talent and the next great story."

—Lisa Cerasoli

7

THE BUSINESS OF STORYTELLING

NOW THAT THE *TELLING* OF your story is completed, how do you go about *selling* it? How do you find your way from a completed and polished story to a deposit into your account? *How do I market my story? Do I need an agent? How do I find someone to represent me? How do I turn storytelling into a lucrative career? Who sends me the check?*

Amateur storytellers become professional by studying what the market buys and by transforming their stories into recognizably commercial properties. Whether you find a representative—agent, manager, or attorney—or not, successful storytellers take full charge of their own marketing. It is, after all, *your* career that's at stake. This chapter outlines the basic marketing equipment a storyteller needs in any storytelling market. Our step-by-step guide to loglines, **sell sheets**, queries, and cover letters focus on the sales principles behind your approach to the story market; plus, we'll give you directions on how to write the various story-selling sales tools, and when and how to use the mail, email, and the telephone.

This chapter presents facts and figures about storytellers—novelists and screenwriters—who've amassed fortunes from their storytelling acumen. We've listed the top-earning storytellers at the end of the book to encourage you to emulate them, and to read them so you can see with your own eyes what it takes to succeed. Suffice it to entice you further that M. Night Shyamalan was paid $7.2 million for *The Village*, $5 million for *Lady in the Water*, $4.7 million for *Unbreakable*, and $4.7 million for *Signs*.

The good news for the aspiring professional storyteller at least for now is that we're living in a world where intellectual property has become more valuable than real property.

The story marketplace in today's world is both complex and simple.

It's complex in that it has myriad outlets and delivery vehicles— methods by which stories are communicated to the public at large.

The simplicity is the constant demand for good stories. All you have to do is find your way into the market.

Amateur storytellers become professional by studying what their **target audience** buys and by transforming their own stories into bona fide literary properties demanded by that market. Becoming a "sold writer" sooner rather than later suggests that you *first* study the form and **genre** that fits your story most closely, *then* learn how to construct your story in the manner applauded by that genre's commercial market. Just as nobody else can be expected to volunteer to correct your grammar and punctuation, nobody else is going to take your "raw story" and turn it into a recognizable shape—unless you pay them for development (www.thewriterslifeline.com is a company that does just that). That's *your* job as an apprentice storyteller, as much as it's a carpenter's job to learn which woods work well as floorboards, which work as cabinetry, and which work to make custom bar stools.

The forms of commercially bought and sold stories include:

- Short stories or **novellas**:
  - Genres include anecdotal, **drabble,** comic, horror, romantics, etc.
- Novels:
  - Genres include romance, thriller, sci-fi, mystery, western, mainstream, etc.
- Children's books:
  - Picture books, first books, fairy tales, issue books, middle grade, Young Adult, etc.
- Song lyrics:
  - Genres include love songs, country, Gospel, rhythm & blues, rock, etc.
- Treatments for feature films, documentary films, or reality series
- Feature screenplays for studio movies or independent movies:
  - Genres include action, comedy, **broad comedy,** action-adventure, thriller, espionage, romantic drama, etc.
- Teleplays for network broadcast or for cable broadcast:
  - Genres include woman in jeopardy, heroic-inspirational, holiday, etc.
- Series or **limited series bibles**, dramatic and reality:
  - Genres include dramatic, sci-fi, social commentary, action, historical, etc.
- Video games:
  - Genres include tactical role-playing, survival-horror, hack and slash, God games, rhythm games, etc.
- Cellphone programs:
  - Genres include educational, sports, games, battles, maps, etc.

Let's start by looking at the primary markets from which stories make their way to today's public:

Publishing and Entertainment

Publishing

Whether your novel or graphic novel is for adults or children, its primary access to the marketplace is through the world of publishing. "Publish" means to "make public," and that is what publishers do— they build a bridge between writers and readers. Today, the world of publishing is clearly divided into *traditional publishing* and *direct publishing*. We are in the midst of a publishing revolution every bit as dramatic as that initiated by Johannes Gutenberg's printing press.

Traditional Publishing

Traditional publishing, sometimes called "**legacy** publishing," is the world in which established publishers like Simon & Schuster, Macmillan, or Penguin Putnam advance money to an author to acquire the right to present his book to the public. It's a model that's been in existence over one hundred years, and though the model is rapidly changing, it is nonetheless still strong, at least when it comes to writers with strong **platforms.**

In today's world, average advances are lower than ever before. This is because of the increased financial risk of releasing stories into a marketplace that is flooded with hundreds of thousands of new titles every year. In fact, it's a general truth that advances are either very high or very low, with the "middle-sized" advance radically rarer than it was ten years ago.

I explain the entire process of submitting your novel to traditional publishers in *How to Publish Your Novel,* published by SquareOne Books, so I won't go into all the details here. Suffice it to say, traditional publishing today is exceedingly difficult for new novelists, especially for males (since the majority of fiction editors are female, and by far the majority of fiction readers are female, as well). It may take you several years to find a legacy publisher to invest in your work. You've already noticed that the display tables at bookstores are loaded with "brand name" authors, whose work may or may not be superior to your own. They have earned their places on the tables by substantial sales and are likely to remain there as long as they have books to publish. That's actually good news for you—once you become a brand, you, too, will retain the loyalty of the publishers, book buyers, and store owners. A brand is a tool used for identifying a person and/or product. It can be a catchphrase, a symbol/logo, or even the product itself.

In the world of traditional publishers, your best bet is to find a representative (agent, attorney, or literary manager) who can take your story to the publishing marketplace. So swamped are the publishers that they are much more likely to take a manuscript seriously if it's been submitted to them by a representative they have done business with before, or at least know by reputation.

Where do you find such a representative? The easiest place, of course, is the internet. Here are some examples and places to get started:

1. www.searchforpublishers.com

This is a website that lets you choose your representative through genre.

2. www.findyourpublisher.com

This one helps you narrow down your publisher search by asking for your genre, your publishing date, and what your overall goals are.

3. www.underdown.org

This website is specifically for finding children's book publishers. It's more limited in its scope than the previous two sites.

4. www.firstwriter.com

This site helps you search for literary agents as well as book publishers.

5. www.agentquery.com

This site is specifically for researching and locating literary agents.

Aside from the internet, we recommend two directories above all others: *Jeff Herman's Guide to Book Publishers, Editors, and Literary Agents 2017: Who They Are! What They Want! And How to Win Them Over!* and *Writer's Market 2017* by Robert Lee Brewer. Both books, easily available at bookstores or online, will lead you not only to representatives, but also directly to publishers. They will tell you what each representative or publisher is looking for, and how to approach them. You'll learn which publishers are open to submissions directly from writers, and which insist that you approach them through representatives. And the best part is, an updated version is published every year, so you can be sure you're using the most current information the market has to offer.

In the world of fiction, you must submit a completed manuscript. Very few publishers have the time or desire to read a partial novel from an unknown novelist. They want to know the novel is complete.

Often, you're allowed to make **multiple submissions** to representatives and publishers, so long as you inform them that your submission is multiple. The directories will tell you if a publisher accepts multiple submissions. If a company does not accept them, just take them off your submission list.

When your book is finally accepted by a traditional publisher, you will receive a contract that allows them to publish the work. If you have not yet acquired a representative, now is the perfect time to do so—contact the rep of your choice and let them know you have an interested publisher and need him or her to negotiate the contract for you. At the very least, ask an entertainment attorney to read and negotiate it, keeping in mind that attorneys can upset deals unless you specifically tell them you want to close. Their job is to improve the contract in your favor as much as the publisher will allow.

Now you've signed your contract. What happens next? It takes anywhere from nine to eighteen months or more for a traditional publisher to put your novel into the marketplace. Each company has a seasonal catalogue listing the books to appear that quarter. Their catalogues go to press approximately six months before the start of a quarter, and, in many cases, the catalogues are set a year in advance. The ample lag allows them the time to market and "sell in" your novel to their network of salespeople and buyers.

Although the traditional publisher will market your novel to some extent, most newly published authors complain about their publishers' lack of marketing. If you're a first-time author, you'll need to support your book with a marketing campaign of your own. Your personal campaign is your *best hope* for garnering attention to your novel. If it begins to succeed, you can expect your publisher to join the bandwagon and accelerate their marketing efforts. But if your personal campaign isn't successful, it's not likely they will put extra effort into your book.

Direct Publishing

More and more novelists are breaking in today by publishing their first novels themselves, primarily via e-book and print on demand (**POD**). Any stigmas attached to this kind of publishing are long forgotten. Even major publishers use POD these days. It's simply a matter of believing in yourself enough to do what's necessary to get your story to your readership. Many companies, like our Story Merchant Books (www.storymerchantbooks.com), are available to assist you in direct publishing our book.

There is one huge caveat to direct publishing: so many books are direct-published *badly*. You are digging your own literary tomb if your novel doesn't stand above the crowd of mediocre millions. More than five thousand books are uploaded and published on Amazon daily— that's just a fact. Most poorly published first novels disappear beneath the vast ocean of approximately 1,825,000 new Amazon titles published each year in the United States alone. What will give your novel a chance to emerge is:

1) a powerful concept that appeals to readers.
2) a professionally-edited story.
3) a professional cover.
4) a marketing plan that will drive readers to your book (see Appendix A for an exemplary Marketing Plan).

Entertainment

Most novelists dream of seeing their stories translated to the screen, whether the television screen or the screen of feature films released in theaters. My *Sell Your Story to Hollywood: Writer's Guide to the Business of Show Business* offers a fully detailed description of the entertainment story market and is recommended reading for those whose stories are dramatic enough to head for the screen.

Just as the publishing world is divided into traditional publishing and direct publishing, today's entertainment world is divided into **major studio motion pictures** and **independent films**.

Major Motion Pictures

Major motion pictures, also known as "Hollywood films," are movies made by the major studios—Columbia Pictures, Walt Disney Studios, 20th Century Fox, Paramount, Universal Pictures, and Warner Bros. For the majors, an average budget today is in the neighborhood of 100 million dollars; it's not unusual for a budget to be over $300 million.

Where studios used to make twenty or more films each year, modern production output has diminished to fewer than a dozen per year. Because the major studios are owned by corporate conglomerates like CBS and Sony, they would rather produce five 200-million-dollar blockbusters that they know will earn money than a dozen lower-budgeted films that are rolls of the dice. This means every single decision, beginning with which movie to make, is dominated by financial considerations.

For that reason, studios almost always acquire a novel—known as an "underlying literary property"—that has a substantial track record in the marketplace, either as a bestseller or as a major critical success. A studio would rather pay a million dollars for the rights to a bestselling novel than twenty thousand for the rights to a great book with no significant commercial track record. A purchase of that size allows them to assign the **adaptation** to a major screenwriter. By the same thinking, they'd rather pay a major screenwriter a million dollars to write the novel's screenplay than pay an unknown screenwriter fifty thousand dollars—even though the latter might very well do a better job in a shorter time. A major screenwriter (like the ones listed at the end of this book) will attract a major director. A major director will attract a major cast. This thinking is why the studios are referred to in shorthand as "the majors."

The major studios make more money from the merchandising that spins off from their blockbusters than they do from the films themselves. Their focus is not on storytelling, but on the consumer behavior that Hollywood storytelling inspires. "Don't ever call me a filmmaker," the head of a major studio told me one night at dinner at his home. "I'm a toymaker who makes films to promote my toys."

But this studio thinking is the very reason you want to get into their game. Once you're in, you're regarded as someone they can pay in six figures. And, if you continue persevering, it may be even more difficult to get out of the game than to get into it in the first place. Getting your story at least distributed, if not produced, by a major is one of the ultimate goals of most ambitious writers. Don't give up on that goal but understand it's more likely to come later in your career—when you've established a name for yourself by writing good stories and getting readers to respond to them. As soon as the studio "trackers" have your story on their radar—like Gillian Flynn's *Gone Girl* or Paula Hawkins' *The Girl on the Train*—it can be snapped up by a major for a significant advance against a purchase price in the millions of dollars. Our client John Scott Shepherd's *Henry's List of Wrongs* was purchased outright by New Line Studios (now part of Warner) for $1.2 million; Steve Alten's *The Meg* was originally purchased by Disney for the same amount—later, by New Line, and ultimately by Warner Brothers.

In Hollywood, five things guarantee success (as I first discussed in *A Writer's Time*):

1. *Perseverance (a.k.a. determination, a.k.a. stamina),* or in Winston Churchill's words: "Never, never, never give up."

2. *Connections.* Stories less exciting or original than yours get made into films every year because the storyteller has developed friends in the business who see the potential of his or her work.

3. *Being fun to work with*. The corollary: Stay off everyone's "Life Is Too Short" list.

4. *Luck a.k.a. Timing*. Sometimes you simply hit the market at the exact right moment for your story, and things move along quickly. Sometimes, alas, you hit the market a tad too late—after several stories similar to yours have been put into production. If that happens, just hold on until the tide changes in your favor.

5. *Talent*. There it is, at last, the characteristic you're banking on. And you should be. If you have talent and can navigate the turbulent river of stories to the produced stories on the other side, you need never cross back to where you are. You'll have their attention and, if you're fun to work with, all the connections you'll need.

It's one of the grand catch-22s in life that your movie can be made if you have *any one* of the characteristics above. Sir Richard Attenborough's *Gandhi* and Steve Alten's *Meg* were made after twenty years of persistence; as was our UP TV movie *Angels in the Snow*, based on Rexanne Becnel's novel. Movies, weak or not, can be the product of the writer having a connection—or of her or him "being fun to work with." And, of course, sheer luck can push a movie into quick production, as it did for our *Joe Somebody*, based on John Scott Shepherd's original script.

But talent is not sufficient. Your story will not be turned into a film just because it's brilliant. Brilliant stories are all too often left by the wayside because their storytellers haven't mastered any one of the first four characteristics.

By the way, since luck and timing play a huge role in the business of show business, do your research before submitting a story and, if the coast looks clear, don't be afraid to mumble pagan chants each morning as you head out to market your story.

Independent Motion Pictures

The good news for those unknown novelists who've written great stories without achieving bestseller status is that independent filmmaking is experiencing an explosive creative and commercial renaissance, the expansion of independent films a response to the major studios' contraction. Watching the Academy Awards of the past few years—in 2010, for example, when *The Hurt Locker* won the Oscar for Best Picture against the 400-million-dollar blockbuster nominee *Avatar*, like *Moonlight* ($4 million) winning over *La La Land* ($30 million)—is exciting confirmation that independent filmmaking is where the greatest creativity lies, and greatest hope for new storytellers. That very well might be because indies also express the greatest heart.

Here, the catch-22 is that screenplays cost money to develop, and development money is the hardest kind to acquire in independent filmmaking. It's rare for an independent producer to have development financing available. Therefore, it's equally rare for the indie to pay significant money to a novelist to option his or her novel—or to pay for a screenwriter to write a screenplay. If he must choose between paying a screenwriter over paying a novelist, the independent producer will naturally do his best to pay the screenwriter—it's the screenplay that can be made into a film, not the novel itself. If a successful producer wants to option your book for little or no advance money, think twice before turning it down. His or her passion may be your best way in.

The novelist's best hope for making his screen dreams come true is having a bestselling novel. Though by itself that's no guarantee, it allows two opportunities for your book: it might be optioned by a major studio, or it might find its way into independent production.

113

If you understand the practical realities of the filmmaking process, you can improve your chances of turning your novel into a film. To reiterate, the first step after acquiring the "dramatic rights" to your novel is to create a professional treatment based on it, one which remedies whatever dramatic problems your novel might pose. The treatment can help you sell your story, but it can also help prospective buyers diagnose any remaining dramatic issues that need to be remedied during the writing of the screenplay.

Then, create that screenplay, if you can. The screenplay is necessary for making a film. We would say writing a good screenplay is maybe ten times more difficult than writing a good novel. For that reason, we generally recommend *against* trying your hand at it unless you've mastered the screenwriter's craft and have a steel-trap objectivity toward your book. Remember, a major motion picture studio would far rather pay a million dollars to have a screenplay written by a successful screenwriter (one whose movies have done very well at the box office) than to save money with an amateur. A bad script is worse than no script at all.

If you have direct access to a screenwriter, pause before asking her to write the screenplay of your novel. No matter how well she writes the screenplay, unless she's an **A-list** writer, it will be almost as hard to get the screenplay read by someone in the world of production as it will to have your novel itself read. Make sure you read your friend's screenplays, comparing them to the screenplays of the most successful movies—which can be downloaded free at www.sfy.ru. If you—and your entertainment attorney—are convinced your screenwriter friend will do a good job, then make a deal with her and move forward. At the least, you'll have taken a significant first step toward production (see Appendix B for a template of an option-purchase agreement).

Peter Jackson was paid $20 million to write and direct a single movie: *King Kong.* In fact, in the twentieth century, IP (intellectual property) became more valuable than real property.

Don't tell us writers aren't valued in this world. Your future can be the pot of gold at the end of the rainbow.

8

DEALING WITH REJECTION

YOU HAVEN'T REALLY COMMITTED TO your writing career until you've moved on from your first rejection. Dealing with a "no" is something to be learned in any new career, and the more worthwhile the career the truer that is. We always like to think there's a big blackboard in the sky with every rejection you're ever going to receive, followed by that "yes" you're dreaming of. The catch-22 on this one: the blackboard is invisible. Given that situation, the only logical way to proceed is to get through all those no's as quickly as you can. Time wasted between learning of a rejection—known in Hollywood, by the way, as a "**pass**"—and re-submitting your story is dream wasted. You can feel anyone you need to, or want to, after every rejection, or after a rejection; but don't let that feeling interfere with getting the story out there again. All the world's best salesmen in every field are masters of rejection.

Some advisors urge you to learn how to turn a rejection into an acceptance. We don't agree. One of the worst things that can happen to you is having the *wrong person* say, "Yes." Isn't that true of personal relationships? The story marketplace is very personal.

At the early stages of my writing career, I papered my guest bathroom with rejection slips—the most extraordinary of which bore a pencil-scribbled "NUTS." My father used that bathroom when he came to visit, and returned to the dinner table and said, "Wow, that's depressing." Then he paused and added, "I'm proud of you. I couldn't take it."

Taking rejection is taking control of your career.

We urge you to use "the odds don't apply to me" as a working mantra when it comes to marketing your stories. Just look at the statistics for successful writers who experienced their share of rejection. Though the information here is primarily gleaned from http://www.litrejections.com/best-sellers-initially-rejected/ the table and conclusions are ours. The first column shows the author's number of rejections (sometimes by agents, sometimes by publishers, sometimes a combination). The right-hand columns show an estimate of sales, and the ratio of millions sold per rejection (MPR). If these writers had listened to their accountant-friends and withheld their energy for fear of the odds, their worlds—and ours—would be very different. Stories do change the world.

5	*Anne of Green Gables*	L. M. Montgomery	50 million sold	10 MPR
5	*Life of Pi*	Yann Martel	Man, Booker Prize; over 10 million copies; major motion picture	2 MPR
12	Harry Potter series	J. K. Rowling	500 million sold; major motion pictures; multiple awards	42 MPR

14	*Twilight* series	Stephenie Myer	17 million sold; 183 weeks on *New York Times* Bestseller List. Major motion pictures.	390,000 copies per rejection
17	*The Princess Diaries*	Meg Cabot	15 million sold; major motion picture	880,000 per rejection
20	*The Shack*	William P. Young	Direct-published; 15 million sold	750,000 per rejection
21	*Catch-22*	Joseph Heller	10 million sold; motion picture; awards	480,000 per rejection
23	*Dune*	Frank Herbert	12 million sold; motion pictures; multiple awards	520,000 per rejection
24	*The Notebook*	Nicholas Sparks	Sold to Time Warner for $1 million; 105 million sold in 50 languages; motion picture	4.375 MPR
27	*And to Think I Saw It on Mulberry Street*	Dr. Seuss	600 million of all his books sold	22.2 MPR
28	*A Time to Kill*	John Grisham	Sales: 250 million; major motion picture	8.9 MPR
30	*The Peter Principle*	Laurence J. Peter	#1 *New York Times* Bestseller; over 1 million sold	333,000 per rejection

31	*The Thomas Berryman Number*	James Patterson	Edgar for Best Novel; bestseller; over $700 million earned	22.8 MPR
38	*Gone with the Wind*	Margaret Mitchell	30 million sold; major motion picture	789,000 per rejection
60	*The Help*	Kathryn Stocked	Over 7 million sold; 100 weeks on *NYT* Bestseller List; published in 35 countries; major motion picture	1.16 MPR
140	*Chicken Soup for the Soul*	Jack Canfield & Mark Victor Hansen	80 million copies sold	570,000 copies per rejection
200	*The Riders of High Rock*	Louis L'Amour	330 million overall sales	660,000 per rejection
500	*The Mysterious Affair at Styles*	Agatha Christi	Overall sales $2 billion+; motion pictures; series	40 MPR

No matter how many rejections you earn, you can bet another successful writer earned more. Wasting time getting depressed after a rejection is your prerogative, but it's clearly just a massive waste of time. The sooner you fall, the sooner you'll get back up and succeed.

"Rejection," like "submission" and "acceptance" is part of the repressive jargon of traditional publishers, evolved to keep writers firmly in their place. When I started selling to Hollywood, it was a pleasant surprise to learn that rejection isn't even part of the vocabulary of an industry that knows damned well that creativity is tough, opinion untrustworthy, and timing everything. One person's rat is another person's lion. Hollywood buyers have a hard time even using the word "pass." More likely they'll say, "Not right for us now, but the door is always open." Or they'll say nothing at all.

How many times can you fail to sell your story?

How many times can you try?

Remember Winston Churchill's "never, never, never...." Never give up is the mantra the determined new writer must embrace. The only closed doors are the ones you shut yourself.

After four romance novels and little success, **Paula Hawkins** sat down and wrote a psychological thriller *The Girl on the Train* over a six-month period. Hawkins had to borrow money from her father to stay afloat while she wrote. The book was released in 2015. By 2016, the movie was filmed and released starring Golden Globe winner Emily Blunt. It has made over $170 million at the box office worldwide. Hawkins is now on the list of world's richest authors, selling over eleven million copies.

9

TURNING AUTHORS INTO FILMMAKERS

BY COMMISSIONING YOUR OWN SCREENPLAY, you become a producer. In recent years, we've been spreading the word: the best hope for novelists determined to see their stories on the screen is for them to *become filmmakers* and produce their own films.

If you believe in your story enough to direct-publish it, why not go to the next level and produce it yourself? If you do, you'll discover that many independent films that make it to the screen began with the writer of the story opening his own wallet and putting her money where her mouth is.

When we enter into a **coproduction deal** with a writer who wants to become a filmmaker, we outline the steps required along the way to put into perspective the amount of footwork it takes to independently produce a film:

1) Write or perfect the screenplay until it becomes a professional **"shooting script."**

2) Choose alternative **locations** for shooting the film that balance financial with artistic considerations.

3) Create a professional production budget that accounts for every single step in the filmmaking process, from development to marketing the finished film.

4) Create a finance, distribution, and marketing plan by which the budget can be put together—taking advantage of:

    a) **"soft money,"** such as **tax rebate incentives** offered by various states and foreign countries;

    b) **presales** of your film to foreign or domestic markets;

    c) actual **equity investment**;

    d) and borrowed money (referred to variously as **gap, mezzanine**, or **bridge** financing) to cover the balance of the budget.

5) Simultaneously create a **"target cast"** that fits within the proposed budget, but at the same time satisfies distributors that the film can be sold in many territories of the world.

6) Attach a **sales agent** who's willing to estimate the presales for the film based on the cast that he or she and the filmmakers mutually approve.

7) Attach a director that the sales agent and cast approve.

8) Attach the lead cast.

9) Create a production schedule that accommodates all of the above.

Of course, this do-it-yourself route is not for the faint of heart. And you can do this smart, or you can do it not so smart. The smart way is to enlist professional help at every stage of the process, to ensure the people that you trust your story to are *more experienced than you are*. In the less-than-smart scenario, they are as inexperienced as you.

But how do you go about enlisting that help? How do you go about building your film? You've got to do your own work and research to prepare. So again, we've listed the step-by-step process below, and this time we've included suggestions on how to give your presentations and film packages the touch of professional air they need to be viewed by professionals who can aid you:

1) Write the screenplay (using professional screenwriting software such as *Final Draft®*—https://www.finaldraft.com/), or get it written and turn it into a professional shooting script. Once you've polished and proofread your story to near perfection, you can utilize **coverage** and analysis services by professional companies to tell you whether or not your script is ready for the market. Companies like The Writer's Lifeline (www.thewriterslifeline.com) and The Black List (www.theblcklst.com) are two such outlets.

2) Choose locations for shooting the film. While a **location scout** will primarily be responsible for this once the project goes into official pre-production, that doesn't mean you shouldn't be thinking about where your story takes place, and what location best represents that place. For years, Hollywood was the go-to place to shoot movies. But now, the possibilities are virtually endless, and you should not only research locations that will advance your story, but locations that are also friendly to your budget. These location suggestions should then be worked into your treatment or film package, along with high-quality sample photos to showcase them. Every state's film commission lists location scouts available in that state.

3) Create a professional production budget. This one can be a bit tricky to do on your own for the first time, which is why a **line producer** will usually be the expert putting the full 100+ page document together. But for starters, you can make a checklist of all the items from development through postproduction that you think will need to be included in the budget of your film. Then you should download or purchase some movie budgeting

software to put those numbers into, like *Movie Magic Budgeting*. Programs like this will also have templates based on types and genres of movies and the various departments, roles, and materials needed to get the movie made. That way you'll have some ideas on where to start. You can also use databases like www.the-numbers.com and www.boxofficemojo.com to look up a film's production budget and get a better idea of where yours fits in and what budgeting categories it needs. Once you've done your research, you can then put the **top sheet** of the budget into your Treatment or Film Package to give potential financers a sense of the overall cost to produce the film. (see Appendix D for a sample budget top sheet)

4) Create a finance, distribution, and marketing plan. Again, this is one best done by professionals, but you should always be thinking about how your story would fare in today's market, and how best to utilize the market to your advantage. Maybe yours is a smaller budget than the studios usually go for, so you'd be better off teaming up with independent production companies. Maybe your financial connections are on a downturn at present, so you can consider using a crowdfunding service, like Kickstarter (www.kickstarter.com) or Indiegogo (www.indiegogo.com). Sometimes, submitting your film to the **festival circuit** is the best way to get exposure, after which time it may be picked up by a distributor. Or you might even consider how it could work as a TV movie or limited-series TV show. It's never so cut and dried as making the movie and then playing it in theaters—there are countless ways for your work to appear on screens these days.

5) Put together a presentation showing your target cast. You've probably always had your ideal cast in mind as you've written your script; the actors you think would be perfect to play the

roles of the characters you've created. While this method is always good for motivation, now is the time to do your research and be realistic about the project. Think about the reality of your budget and let that help you choose actors that can play the role and appeal to a wide audience while still staying within your budget. You may need to reconsider your characters in ways you haven't thought of before. Movie and cast databases that keep track of average and total revenues that actors have made are great resources. Again, check out www.the-numbers.com and www.boxofficemojo.com for starters. Www.imdb.com will also show you an actor's current "STAR meter," or rating, within the industry—this can help you determine how in-demand they are. It will also let you see what upcoming projects actors have, so you'll know right off the bat if they're free, or if they might be tied up for the next five years. Often, the director or other producers will have cast preferences and connections he or she can bring to the table. It's important to be open-minded in circumstances like this.

6) Attach the sales agent. This is another one that you'll want to turn to your directories and guidebooks for. *The Insider's Guide to Independent Film Distribution* by Stacey Parks is a good resource to utilize. Like literary managers or agents, sales agents have preferences for what they're looking to sell, usually based on past experience and current market analysis. But don't leave all that research up to them—if you do your own research ahead of time, you'll be that much more in-the-know about which agents to bring your work to, and you'll be one step closer to your sale.

7) Attach the director. Much like prepping your target cast list, you should also prepare an ideal director list to include in your presentation packages. And you guessed it—research is the

name of the game. Watch films with genres, tones, and styles like your envisioned film, then research the directors of those films. The Directors Guild of America lists 16,000 members at https://www.dga.org/The-Guild/Members. And, again, use IMDb to see what their future production schedules are like. You can sign up for and utilize an IMDbPro account (www.pro-labs.imdb.com), which has even more details on talent and crew credits and schedules. It's a paid subscription service but it's well worth it because it also gives you access to management and contact information for many people in the industry. Narrow your director list down to a few you think can get the job done, have the availability, and are friendly to your budget. Attaching a director can often start to open numerous other production doors for you, especially if they're established in the industry already.

8) Attach the lead cast. The same guidelines that went along with attaching your target cast apply here, but the biggest difference you'll want to keep in mind for your lead role is that they should hold some higher merit and value than the supplemental cast. Strive to attach a name that will entice and excite people—for some, your lead cast will be *the* reason they watch your film. But again, be smart and realistic; you should consider someone who can not only play the role but will appeal to as wide an audience possible, based on age, ethnicity, nationality, etc., all while still fitting within your budget. And don't forget to consider your target's interests and schedule. Again, this is a role that the director will likely want to have a hand in deciding, and you should welcome their suggestions and connections.

9) Create a **production timeline**. This one comes last because you can't do it until all the other pieces have fallen into place. But you can certainly create a timeline that outlines your ideal

127

projection from pre-production to release. This is also something you should include at the end of your treatment or package so that people will have the same general sense of the project that you do. Just keep in mind that things happen and timelines constantly change, as it always seems to go in this industry. Just try to go with the flow, and never let big changes discourage you!

Yes, it is a long and somewhat daunting list and the devil is in the details. The road to the screen may be long and complicated but all worthwhile goals are challenging. The challenge is exactly what makes them worth accomplishing.

Television

Is seeing your story on television an easier path to the screen dream? Not at all. In fact, more money is made by far from television stories than from feature films. The competition in that world couldn't be greater. *Everyone* wants in, and it's a very *small* world. In television, success breeds success, success breeds riches, riches breed more riches, and the people who succeed have a vested interest in retaining their positions.

A few years ago, hundreds of TV movies were being made by both the free networks and pay cable broadcasters. Stories that did not work as studio films or independent movies often had a chance of selling to television—especially stories with female leads, since they were preferred by television's largely female audience.

But that's history. Today, television movies are fewer and farther between, and with lower budgets. Reality programming has taken many of the time slots once allocated to movies. This leaves original stories to find homes in the even more competitive world of dramatic series and limited series.

You'd think that original series dramas might be in demand. They are indeed, but the demand usually focuses on storytellers who've already succeeded in television. Those writers are known as **showrunners.** Studio head Joe Roth once remarked, "An original idea is something that hasn't already been on television." But his remark was intentionally misleading. He wasn't praising originality; he was saying there's no such thing.

An "original idea," in television terms, is an idea that takes a new angle on a character or story that's already proved to attract television audiences. Instead of *The Firm*, which takes place in the world of courts and lawyers, we get *ER*, in the world of hospitals and doctors.

If you have exactly such a story in mind, the best chance you have for selling it today is to partner with a showrunner because he or she has experience in running successful shows. Showrunners come in two varieties: those with infinite ideas, and those who need ideas or true stories to spark their creativity. Your easiest way in is on the coattails of one of the second variety.

Of course, that is another catch-22. Why would a successful showrunner, like Shonda Rhimes, *need* your story idea? She's gotten to where she is because she has good ideas. Most of the time, she wouldn't need your idea, and she also wouldn't want a partner when she can continue succeeding without one.

That rare exception is where the newcomer has a chance. Sometimes, a network or cable company approaches a successful showrunner and asks him to come in for a pitch because they'd love to be in business with him. And sometimes the successful showrunner doesn't have an idea that happens to fit that buyer at the moment.

In this situation, a newcomer with a perfect idea for that buyer may suddenly become attractive to the showrunner. If you're fortunate enough to be on the spot, the best you can reasonably hope for is to share the showrunner's credit. He will take over the story from the moment he agrees to it, but you will ride along as the co-creator (the Writers Guild of America's official designation for the originators of a dramatic show). If you're fortunate enough to have this happen to you, celebrate! It's your entry into the world you've been aspiring to. If you and the showrunner hit it off, you may end up writing some of the episodes in your own show. If they're well received, you may even become an executive producer, as several of my students and clients did for major shows. From there, you may become recognized as a showrunner yourself.

To get to this point, you need to have written the bible for your proposed television series. In some cases, you'll also need what's known as the pilot script, the screenplay version of the first story in the series, which establishes the series' agenda and characters. What these tools are—the bible and the pilot—are described in full detail in my and Chi-Li Wong's *Writing Treatments That Sell: How to Create and Market Your Story Ideas to the Motion Picture and TV Industry, Second Edition*. That book tells you how to turn your story, whether it's original or whether it's your published or unpublished novel, into a treatment—the basic and primary marketing tool for storytellers in the entertainment marketplace. Appendix C shows you what a typical bible looks like.

Other Markets for Stories

In addition to publishing and entertainment, other, more specialized markets for stories include the "**legitimate stage**" (where stories are known as "plays"), music (where stories are known as "songs"), the world of games, and the digital world, where stories of various shapes and sizes get to their audiences by internet download, cellphone, and reading devices like iPads, Kindle readers, and Nooks. So specialized are these worlds that storytellers desiring to enter one need to find a book appropriate to that market.

No matter which story world fits you, you'll need three basic story sales tools.

1—The Pitch Line a.k.a. Logline a.k.a. One-liner

Sometimes referred to as the "**one-liner**," "**logline**," or the "elevator **pitch**," this is the shortest effective presentation of your story that communicates in an enticing way *what it's about*. Here are some examples.

A bounty hunter and a mafia accountant, locked together in a cross-country delivery, discover they have more in common than either could ever have imagined (*Midnight Run*).

A war widow waits fifty years for her MIA husband to honor his promise to return to her on Valentine's Day (*The Lost Valentine*).

Three generations of New Orleans madams face down the FBI— and win (*The Madam's Family*).

A Seattle television anchor has to choose between following her dream to New York or finding her heart at home (*Life or Something Like It*).

What happens when a fish out of water is a mermaid (*Splash!*)?

He was left behind. On Mars (*The Martian*).

Notice that there are no wasted words, no buildup or conclusion, such as "in my story" or "this is a story that" or "and that's what the story is about." The pitch is direct, compelling, and to the point.

The purpose of the pitch line is to capture initial attention. The ideal response from your prospect (editor, agent, producer, attorney) is, "Tell me more." To answer, you would send the sell sheet.

2—The Sell Sheet a.k.a. One-pager a.k.a. Overview

The sell sheet is a one-page pitch (**overview**) for your story, focusing on its highlights and broad strokes. Like the pitch line, its purpose is to get your prospect to ask for more. It should be completely positive and compelling, with no qualifications like, "keep in mind, this is my first story," or "I can't begin to tell you everything in a few words." The best way to describe the **one-pager** is to show you a few examples.

Note that the sell sheet includes a teaser and logline as well.

Mirror Image by Dennis Palumbo
(published by Poisoned Pen Press)

LOGLINE: A murder targeting the protagonist accidentally kills the protagonist's patient who, infatuated with him, stole his leather jacket.

PITCH: Mirror Image is a complex psycho thriller of suspense, the first in a series of thrillers featuring Dr. Daniel Rinaldi, a psychologist who consults with the Pittsburgh Police. Rinaldi's specialty is treating victims of violent crime—those who've survived armed robbery, kidnapping, etc., but whose traumatic experience still haunts them.

Kevin Merrick, a college student and victim of an armed assault, is one of these people. A fragile, troubled kid desperate for a role model and a sense of identity, Kevin has begun dressing like Rinaldi, mirroring his appearance. Before Daniel has a chance to work through this with his patient, he finds Kevin brutally murdered. Stunned, he and the police suspect that he, Rinaldi, had been the intended target.

Feeling responsible, Rinaldi is determined to help find the killer, who's begun leaving death threats for the psychologist. And when Kevin Merrick's identity as the estranged son of a Bill Gates-like biotech giant is revealed, the investigation of his murder turns into a national story…even as another person turns up dead.

CONCEPT: A page-turning novel of suspense and intrigue, Mirror Image weaves together a puzzling mystery full of unexpected twists, and an intense, erotic love story. It introduces us to a diverse, compelling cast of characters whose lives and concerns engage us and will continue to engage as they unfold in the books to come.

WRITER: The author is a well-known Los Angeles industry psychologist, with a platform that includes a regular column in *The Huffington Post*.

Nobody Walks by Dennis Walsh

LOGLINE: An attorney goes incognito into the San Fernando Valley's porn and drugs underworld to track down and bring to justice the murderers of his kid brother.

PITCH: The only son of a large Irish-American family to stay on the straight and narrow, Dennis Walsh is a small-time lawyer living on the fringes of the legal establishment, just managing to get by. But when his kid brother, Christopher, is found stuffed in a trash barrel in a storage locker in Van Nuys, California, the burden of the Walsh family name comes crashing down around him again.

Dennis's brother Tim arrives for the funeral, but he's not just there to say goodbye—he won't rest until those responsible for Christopher's death are in the ground with him. If Dennis wants to find Christopher's killers without losing another brother, he must slink between his life as a stand-up lawyer and hitting the streets to try and convince the dopers, thieves, prostitutes, porn stars, and jailbirds that populated Christopher's world to come forward and cooperate with the police.

133

But it's not so easy. Tim is ready to do anything to avenge his brother—that includes cracking skulls and firing off more than warning shots. It comes down to a fight between doing things Dennis's way, or the "Walsh family" way. Dennis becomes a reluctant sheriff on the streets and at home, doing all he can to keep Tim in check while still trying to build a case where the police can't. Or just won't. Even prosecutors continuously tell him he's jeopardizing not only the case, but his life.

Staying on the right side of the law to hunt down the murderers puts every part of Dennis to the test, and it doesn't take long before the brother who went clean must get his hands dirty. With the gravity of a Scorsese film, this classic yet gritty tale transcends the true crime genre. Nobody Walks is the harrowing story of a family, brothers, and the true meaning of justice.

CONCEPT: In the vein of *The Boondock Saints* and *Chinatown* comes this true crime memoir of brotherly love and vengeance.

WRITER: Dennis Walsh continues to practice law in the San Fernando Valley. This is his true story.

Raptor from the thriller *Fossil River* by Jock Miller

LOGLINE: Dinosaurs and oil have an ageless affinity: to create oil, dinosaurs must die.

PITCH: The Noatak National Preserve in northern Alaska has become home to a threatening new predator that leaves only cleanly stripped moose carcasses behind as evidence of its existence. It's also home to a newly discovered, magnificently huge oil field deep underground—one that the government will stop at nothing to exploit. Repeated warnings

134

of the new Park danger from Ranger Scott Chandler do nothing to heed their drive.

Desperate for answers, Chandler summons brilliant archaeologist Dr. Kim Fulton to the Preserve. After a risky convoy deep into the forest, she confirms that Deinonychus, a prehistoric lethal predator capable of effortlessly slashing through flesh, has emerged from beneath recently melted glaciers in the heart of the Preserve, and they'll do anything to protect their nest—which sits right on top of the oil field. Despite the deinos literally ripping a team of scientists to pieces, the military convoy that arrives at the Preserve doesn't flinch—they'll blow up every deino to get to that oil if they must.

Chandler, Kim, and some unexpected allies must find a way to convince the military to back down before they destroy what is possibly the greatest natural discovery of all time. But they've got to decide what they're willing to risk to do so—and fast.

CONCEPT: What if the world's largest fossil fuel deposit is found in Alaska's Glacier National Park as the nation's lights are about to extinguish? But preventing access to the oil, a colony of living fossil dinosaurs will protect its territory to the death.

WRITER: Jock Miller received a BS degree in Zoology from Ohio Wesleyan University. Focus of study: paleontology, ornithology, and comparative anatomy. He attended Harvard Business School to participate in a case study publishing management program sponsored by the American Business Press. Miller has appeared on cable TV talk shows, been interviewed on numerous radio talk shows including Barbara Walters', and has been a guest lecturer at C.W. Post College and C.W. Post Brentwood Campus, lecturing on industry's responsibility to society and its community.

Note that these sample pitches are various lengths, but all are brief. They provide an overview, not all-inclusive details, of the stories they're selling.

3—The Treatment

Once you've constructed your log-line and your one-pager, the last piece of the writer's selling arsenal is the treatment. In *Writing Treatments That Sell,* Chi-Li Wong and I describe in detail exactly how to write a treatment for the various markets. The treatment is a way to present the full scope of your story, and a most useful diagnostic tool in the creative process. Writing a treatment can save you months of false starts and dead ends, because it allows you to detect story problems in a format that you're not invested in emotionally, as you might be with your screenplay.

Most buyers prefer to be approached by email rather than telephone or snail mail. First, send the pitch line and wait for a response. Since no response may mean a number of things, send the pitch line again in two weeks. If you receive a response, it'll either be "not for us" (or a variation) or "love to hear more" (or something similar). Now is the time to send the sell sheet, a treatment, or both.

Here's a general list of the vital ingredients from *Writing Treatments That Sell* that comprise a rock-star treatment:

- Start your treatment with a log-line and short pitch that hooks the reader.
- A treatment is a loose narrative of your story told in acts (usually three acts for a feature).

- Treatments are generally five-to-twenty-five pages long. A producer should be able to read it efficiently, effortlessly, and be engaged throughout.
- Drama is at every turn in a treatment. Every next scene, even in comedic treatments, must have conflict—dramatic twists and turns—without resolution until the climax of the story. This is a key difference in a treatment and screenplay, as compared to a novel.
- Don't get fancy with the language in a treatment. Clarity is the goal.

Treatments are highly visual. Films are 80 percent visual, so it stands to reason a treatment and script need to have clear imagery. A treatment's lifespan is brief in Hollywood, but it serves an important purpose—to sell a story. They're a roadmap to writing the script for that story, and they're read more often and with more ease than a 300-page novel or even a 100-page screenplay from an unknown writer. Even when you talk a producer into reading your novel, you can't guarantee he or she will have your vision—see the film or series as you do in your mind. With a treatment already adapted from your book, the "envisioning" of the blockbuster hit has been done for them, dramatically increasing your odds of selling your story to Hollywood.

Tim Crothers, former senior writer at *Sports Illustrated*, authored *The Queen of Katwe*, a true story about the Ugandan junior woman chess master, Phiona Mutesi. The book was expanded from his award-winning article and published in 2015. The movie was released in 2016.

10

HOW DO I PROTECT MY STORY UNTIL I'M PAID FOR IT?

EVERY NOVICE STORYTELLER IS WORRIED about "protection," and in this internet era of viral communication, the worry is often justified. Urging practical caution in the business of storytelling, this chapter presents both dangers and solutions. Publishing your story on the internet for free, for example, may seem like a quick way to get readers; but storytellers need to be aware that internet publication, if not done professionally, is an irreversible compromise to their ability to profit from their own copyrights. Once it's up there free, it will be hard to place it with a publisher or production company wanting to acquire its copyright.

The two primary ways to protect your story are (1) registration of its copyright with the Library of Congress Registrar of Copyrights and (2) registration with the Writers Guild of America.

Copyrighting and registering are two separate actions.

Copyrighting occurs the moment you have written your words. You don't have to use the © symbol to let the world know you own your story. By law, you own your work when you write it, and anyone who uses it for their own without getting your permission is misappropriating your copyright.

Registration, on the other hand, is a recording system created to help you *prove* that the story is yours.

Registering your copyright can be done online by transmitting your story with a statement that it is yours and paying a registration fee. Should you find yourself in court against someone who claims the story is his instead of yours, your ability to produce the registration may be definitive proof that your claim proceeds his. Registration proves only that you filed the claim that the story is yours. But, in the absence of an earlier claim filed by another party, it is your best defense.

Register your novel at http://www.copyrightregistry-online-form.com.

If you're a screenwriter, you can also register your screenplay, teleplay, treatment, novel, or nonfiction book with the Writers Guild of America/West, http://www.wgawregistry.org/webrss/, which has the same effect as registering it with the Copyright Office.

One or the other is all you need to do.

Then, we'd recommend you put the whole business of protection out of your mind and concentrate on polishing your story and getting it to market.

"Don't self-publish. You'll kill your writing career before it begins."

Those were the words of the last agent to turn *Still Alice* down. Neuroscientist **Lisa Genova** direct-published anyway. One year later, *Still Alice* sold at auction to Simon & Schuster for half a million dollars. In January of 2009, *Still Alice* became a *New York Times* bestseller and remained on that chart for over forty weeks. Today there are over a million copies in print and it's translated into twenty-five different languages. Julianne Moore won the Academy Award for Best Actress in the 2014 film adaptation.

But it wasn't just about the book. Genova spent a year marketing on every online platform possible, including managing her own website and blog and scheduling at least two book events per month. Seven months into her self-marketing platform, she hired publicists, who further assisted her in gaining traction with television, radio, newspapers, blogs, book clubs, and Amazon reviewers.

Winning book awards along the way didn't hurt, either.

EPILOGUE

BEFORE THE INVENTION OF WRITING, stories were transmitted from person to person, household to household, city to city, and kingdom to kingdom through the highly-efficient but limited oral tradition—word of mouth was memory's highest expression sung or chanted from court to campfire by itinerant storytellers (bards, troubadours, minnesingers, jongleurs, minstrels, etc.) weaving their spells over audiences whose values and thoughts were shaped by their heroic or cautionary tales.

Humanity needed stories so much it couldn't trust the new inventions—cuneiform tablets, parchment scrolls, or papyrus—to memorialize them permanently. They could be destroyed by innocent or malicious hands—the oral tradition remained; it was truly eternal.

With the coming of the alphabet and writing, the narrative epic tradition soon evolved into drama. The ancient Greek Great Dionysian Festival was held annually in the theater at Epidaurus. Citizens attended the three-day event to re-live together the myth upon which the culture of the city was founded. The audience became lightly inebriated at these events so that the boundaries of identity that separated social classes were broken down—and the event became a communal experience.

Playwrights, directors, and actors became the new storytellers, and were, like the bards before them, considered demigods. They were commissioned by wealthy patrons—and by the gods themselves to whom the plays were dedicated—to impart stories with powerful themes to audiences hungry for meaning in a chaotic world. Such was the power of the storyteller to transport the audience.

As writing became more widespread and trusted, libraries were established to preserve laboriously hand-copied manuscripts that proliferated throughout the world of the refined.

The late nineteenth century saw the advent of telegraph and radio, even more efficient ways to spread stories and information publicly. The same period brought the telephone, which allowed stories to spread privately throughout the world instead. Both media were a throwback to the oral tradition, since the stories spread by radio and telephone arrived at the audience's ears, rather than their eyes, and were in the shape of invisible electrons, instead of printed words and letters that could be easily reviewed. It was the oral tradition with restrictions of place eliminated.

The tape recorder and other sound-recording devices quickly followed to change it all again, and the teletype allowed information and stories to become fixed records, instead of the recipient's memories of what he'd heard on the radio or over the phone.

Starting in the earliest years of the twentieth century, most of the world now has the inspirational power of stories conveyed through television and cinema. Moving pictures, along with their sister, music, have become our "global language"—with the most-watched annual live television performance being the Academy Awards, with the Emmys following close behind.

With the dominance of the internet, beginning in the late twentieth century, humanity invented perhaps the ultimate way of preserving stories as we approach a point where all information and all stories will be accessible to all audiences in cyberspace. Not to mention, smartphones make storytelling both literal and visual at the same time—and don't get us started on texting!

As a storytelling vehicle, film and all its descendants transcend the written word as moving pictures transcend hieroglyphics that must be deciphered. The picture goes straight to the heart, without the need for translation through the mind's structures of logic. In effect, we've recreated the conditions of classical Greek theater, using the intensity of sound, light, and darkness to transport ourselves out of our workaday minds—out of logical time, into mythical time—so that filmmakers now function as the new priests of dramatic religion. That's why getting a story onto the big screen is the ultimate dream of most writers.

Motion pictures are a collection of exemplary tales reflecting our deepest as well as our most superficial, lowest as well as highest, dreams. They mirror the times we live. A picture—digitally transmitted via internet or smartphone—is worth ten thousand words, and the pictorial images stay with us long after most of the dialogue fades. If *words* were the most important elements of a great story, Paul Coelho's *The Alchemist* would not be the most translated book of any living author. When a book is translated the words change—only the story remains. In 1988, when Coelho took two weeks out of his life to write *The Alchemist*, he knew he had something. (*"The book just wrote itself!"*) Today, *The Alchemist* has been translated into sixty-eight languages in 150 countries. It is a universal story written in the universal language of scenes and images, and it is simply understood. No wonder it has spent hundreds of weeks on the *New York Times* Bestseller List and has been a bestselling book for twenty years.

Welcome to the visionary company that maintains the storytelling tradition! Serve it well with your serious dedication to the craft.

OUR FAVORITE NOVELS

The novels listed here run the gamut of commercial success, but all are truly classics worth your time to read—and to study the storytelling:

- *1984* (George Orwell)
- *Absalom, Absalom!* (William Faulkner)
- *Adventures of Huckleberry Finn* (Mark Twain)
- *The Adventures of Tom Sawyer* (Mark Twain)
- *Advise and Consent* (Allen Drury)
- *The Alexandrian Quartet* (Lawrence Durrell)
- *Alice in Wonderland* (Lewis Carroll)
- *Anna Karenina* (Leo Tolstoy)
- *Are you there, God? It's me, Margaret.* (Judy Blume)
- *As I Lay Dying* (William Faulkner)
- *The Ballad of the Sad Café* (Carson McCullers)
- *Being There* (Jerzy Kosińksi)
- *Birdy* (William Wharton)
- *Bleak House* (Charles Dickens)
- *The Book Thief* (Markus Zusak)
- *Brave New World* (Aldous Huxley)
- *The Brothers Karamazov* (Fyodor Dostoevsky)
- *Candide* (Voltaire)
- *Cat's Cradle* (Kurt Vonnegut)
- *Catch-22* (Joseph Heller)

- *The Catcher in the Rye* (J. D. Salinger)
- *Charlie Boy* (Peter S. Feibleman)
- *Childhood's End* (Arthur C. Clarke)
- *A Clockwork Orange* (Anthony Burgess)
- *The Color Purple* (Alice Walker)
- *A Confederacy of Dunces* (John Kennedy Toole)
- *Crime and Punishment* (Fyodor Dostoevsky)
- *Cry, the Beloved* Country (Alan Paton)
- *The Curious Incident of the Dog in the Night-time* (Mark Haddon)
- *Damage* (Josephine Hart)
- *The Dark Half* (Stephen King)
- *David Copperfield* (Charles Dickens)
- *The Day of the Jackal* (Frederick Forsyth)
- *The Day of the Locust* (Nathanael West)
- *Death in Venice* (Thomas Mann)
- *The Death of Artemio Cruz* (Carlos Fuentes)
- *The Deep End of the Ocean* (Jacquelyn Mitchard)
- *Don Quixote* (Miguel de Cervantes)
- *Doctor Zhivago* (Boris Pasternak)
- *Dracula* (Bram Stoker)
- *Dune* (Frank Herbert)
- *Eleanor & Park* (Rainbow Rowell)
- *Ender's Game* (Orson Scott Card)
- *The English Patient* (Michael Ondaatje)
- *The Exorcist* (William Peter Blatty)
- *Fahrenheit 451* (Ray Bradbury)
- *The Fall of the House of Usher* (Edgar Allan Poe)
- *Fight Club* (Chuck Palahniuk)
- *The Firm* (John Grisham)

- *For Whom the Bell Tolls* (Ernest Hemingway)
- *The Fountainhead* (Ayn Rand)
- *Frankenstein* (Mary Shelley)
- *Gargantua and Pantagruel* (François Rabelais)
- *The Glass Castle* (Jeannette Wells)
- *A God Against the Gods* (Allen Drury)
- *The Gods Themselves* (Isaac Asimov)
- *The Golden Bowl* (Henry James)
- *Gone with the Wind* (Margaret Mitchell)
- *The Grapes of Wrath* (John Steinbeck)
- *The Great Gatsby* (F. Scott Fitzgerald)
- *Gulliver's Travels* (Jonathan Swift)
- *Hawaii* (James Michener)
- *The Heart Is a Lonely Hunter* (Carson McCullers)
- *Heart of Darkness* (Joseph Conrad)
- *The Heart of the Matter* (Graham Greene)
- *Heartbeat* (Sharon Creech)
- *Heartburn* (Nora Ephron)
- *The Hobbit* (J. R. R. Tolkien)
- *Of Human Bondage* (W. Somerset Maugham)
- *The Hunchback of Notre-Dame* (Victor Hugo)
- *If Beale Street Could Talk* (James Baldwin)
- *The Immoralist* (André Gide)
- *Invisible Man* (Ralph Ellison)
- *Interview with the Vampire* (Anne Rice)
- *Ivanhoe* (Sir Walter Scott)
- *Jane Eyre* (Charlotte Brontë)
- *A Journal of the Plague Year* (Daniel Defoe)
- *To Kill a Mockingbird* (Harper Lee)

- *Lady Chatterley's Lover* (D. H. Lawrence)
- *The Left Hand of Darkness* (Ursula K. Le Guin)
- *The Life and Opinions of Tristram Shandy, Gentleman* (Laurence Sterne)
- *Life of Pi* (Yann Martel)
- *Light in August* (William Faulkner)
- *The Lightning Thief* (Rick Riordan)
- *Like Water for Chocolate* (Laura Esquivel)
- *The Lion, the Witch, and the Wardrobe* (C.S. Lewis)
- *The Little Prince* (Antoine de Saint-Exupéry)
- *Little Women* (Louisa May Alcott)
- *Lolita* (Vladimir Nabokov)
- *The Lord of the Rings* (J. R. R. Tolkien)
- *Lost in the Sun* (Lisa Graff)
- *Love in the Time of Cholera* (Gabriel García Márquez)
- *Madame Bovary* (Gustave Flaubert)
- *The Magic Mountain* (Thomas Mann)
- *The Magus* (John Fowles)
- *The Marriages Between Zones Three, Four and Five* (Doris Lessing)
- *The Member of the Wedding* (Carson McCullers)
- *Of Mice and Men* (John Steinbeck)
- *The Outsiders* (S.E. Hinton)
- *Middlemarch* (George Eliot)
- *Les Misérables* (Victor Hugo)
- *Miss Lonelyhearts* (Nathanael West)
- *Moby-Dick* (Herman Melville)
- *The Mortgaged Heart* (Carson McCullers)
- *The Moviegoer* (Walker Percy)
- *Mr. Blue* (Myles Connolly)

- *Mrs. Dalloway* (Virginia Woolf)
- *The Name of the Rose* (Umberto Eco)
- *Nausea* (Jean-Paul Sartre)
- *Notes of a Native Son* (James Baldwin)
- *The Old Curiosity Shop* (Charles Dickens)
- *The Old Man and the Sea* (Ernest Hemingway)
- *One Flew Over the Cuckoo's Nest* (Ken Kesey)
- *One Hundred Years of Solitude* (Gabriel García Márquez)
- *A Passage to India* (E. M. Forster)
- *The Picture of Dorian Gray* (Oscar Wilde)
- *The Plague* (Albert Camus)
- *A Portrait of the Artist as a Young Man* (James Joyce)
- *Pride and Prejudice* (Jane Austen)
- *The Prince and the Pauper* (Mark Twain)
- *The Prince of Tides* (Pat Conroy)
- *The Remains of the Day* (Kazuo Ishiguro)
- *Remembrance of Things Past* (Marcel Proust)
- *A Room with a View* (E. M. Forster)
- *The Scarlet Letter* (Nathaniel Hawthorne)
- *The Second Coming* (Walker Percy)
- *The Secret Life of Bees* (Sue Monk Kidd)
- *Sense and Sensibility* (Jane Austen)
- *The Shadow of the Wind* (Carlos Ruiz Zafón)
- *She* (H. Rider Haggard)
- *Siddhartha* (Thomas Mann)
- *Slaughterhouse-Five* (Kurt Vonnegut)
- *Solaris* (Stanislaw Lem)
- *Sons and Lovers* (D. H. Lawrence)
- *The Sound and the Fury* (William Faulkner)

- *The Stranger* (Albert Camus)
- *A Tale of Two Cities* (Charles Dickens)
- *Their Eyes Were Watching God* (Zora Neale Hurston)
- *The Time Traveler's Wife* (Audrey Niffenegger)
- *The Three Musketeers* (Alexandre Dumas)
- *The Three-Body Problem* (Liu Cixin)
- *Thousand Cranes* (Yasunari Kawabata)
- *Through the Looking-Glass* (Lewis Carroll)
- *The History of Tom Jones, a Foundling* (Henry Fielding)
- *Too Late the Phalarope* (Alan Paton)
- *The Trial* (Franz Kafka)
- *Tuesdays with Morrie* (Mitch Albom)
- *The Turn of the Screw* (Henry James)
- *The Unbearable Lightness of Being* (Milan Kundera)
- *Vanity Fair* (William Makepeace Thackeray)
- *White Oleander* (Janet Fitch)
- *The Wind in the Willows* (Kenneth Grahame)
- *Wonder* (R. J. Palacio)
- *Wuthering Heights* (Emily Brontë)
- *Zorba the Greek* (Nikos Kazantzakis)

OUR FAVORITE ORIGINAL SCREENPLAYS

The screenplays listed here include both major studio films and independent movies, but we highly recommend all to you for studying the art of the script:

- *50/50* (Will Reiser)
- *Alien* (Dan O'Bannon)
- *Almost Famous* (Cameron Crowe)
- *Amélie* (Guillaume Laurant and Jean-Pierre Jeunet)
- *American Beauty* (Alan Ball)
- *American Graffiti* (George Lucas, Gloria Katz, and Willard Huyck)
- *American History X* (David McKenna)
- *Angel Eyes* (Gerald DiPego)
- *Annie Hall* (Woody Allen and Marshall Brickman)
- *The Apartment* (Billy Wilder and I.A.L. Diamond)
- *Après Vous* (Benoît Graffin, David Léotard, and Pierre Salvadori, based on an idea by Danièle Dubroux)
- *The Artist* (Michel Hazanavicius)
- *Avatar* (James Cameron)
- *Basic Instinct* (Joe Eszterhas)
- *Being John Malkovich* (Charlie Kaufman)
- *Beverly Hills Cop* (Daniel Petrie, Jr.)
- *The Big Lebowski* (Ethan Coen and Joel Coen)
- *Blue Jasmine* (Woody Allen)
- *Boogie Nights* (Paul Thomas Anderson)

- *Breakfast Club* (John Hughes)
- *Broadcast News* (James L. Brooks)
- *Bulworth* (Warren Beatty and Jeremy Pikser)
- *Burnt by the Sun* (Rustam Ibragimbekov and Nikita Mikhalkov)
- *Butch Cassidy and the Sundance Kid* (William Goldman)
- *The Cake Eaters* (Jayce Bartok)
- *Chinatown* (Robert Towne)
- *Cinema Paradiso* (Giuseppe Tornatore and Vanna Paoli)
- *Close Encounters of the Third Kind* (Steven Spielberg)
- *Clueless* (Amy Heckerling)
- *The Concubine* (Yoon-Jung Hwang, Dae-Seung Kim and Mi-jung Kim)
- *The Crying Game* (Neil Jordan)
- *Deconstructing Harry* (Woody Allen)
- *Departures* (Kundô Koyama)
- *Down with Love* (Eve Ahlert and Dennis Drake)
- *Eat Drink Man Woman* (Ang Lee, James Schamus, and Hui-Ling Wang)
- *E.T. the Extra-Terrestrial* (Melissa Mathison)
- *Exotica* (Atom Egoyan)
- *Face/Off* (Mike Werb and Michael Colleary)
- *Fargo* (Joel Coen and Ethan Coen)
- *Fatso* (Anne Bancroft)
- *The Fighter* (Eric Johnson, Scott Silver, and Paul Tamasy)
- *Four Weddings and a Funeral* (Richard Curtis)
- *The Full Monty* (Simon Beaufoy)
- *Get Shorty* (Scott Frank)
- *Gloomy Sunday* (Ruth Toma and Rolf Schübel)
- *As Good as It Gets* (Mark Andrus and James L. Brooks)
- *Good Will Hunting* (Matt Damon and Ben Affleck)

- *The Goodbye Girl* (Neil Simon)
- *Good Luck Chuck* (Sterling Johnston)
- *Groundhog Day* (Danny Rubin and Harold Ramis)
- *Hard Candy* (Brian Nelson)
- *Harold and Maude* (Colin Higgins)
- *Hot Fuzz* (Edgar Wright and Simon Pegg)
- *Hysteria* (Stephan Dyer, Jonah Lisa Dyer, and Howard Gensler)
- *Ikiru* (Akira Kurosawa, Shinobu Hashimoto, and Hideo Oguni)
- *Innocent Voices* (Luis Mandoki and Oscar Orlando Torres)
- *Inside Job* (Charles Ferguson)
- *Jerry Maguire* (Cameron Crowe)
- *Juno* (Diablo Cody)
- *The King's Speech* (David Seidler)
- *La La Land* (Damien Chazelle)
- *Lars and the Real Girl* (Nancy Oliver)
- *Life Is Beautiful* (Roberto Benigni and Vincenzo Cerami)
- *Little Miss Sunshine* (Michael Arndt)
- *The Lives of Others* (Florian Henckel von Donnersmarck)
- *Love Actually* (Richard Curtis)
- *Mad Max* (George Miller and James McCausland)
- *Magnolia* (Paul Thomas Anderson)
- *Manhattan* (Woody Allen and Marshall Brickman)
- *Me and You and Everyone We Know* (Miranda July)
- *Michael* (Nora Ephron, Delia Ephron, Peter Dexter, and Jim Quinlan)
- *Midnight in Paris* (Woody Allen)
- *Midnight Run* (George Gallo)
- *Monster's Ball* (Milo Addica and Will Rokos)
- *Moonstruck* (John Patrick Shanley)

- *My Best Friend's Wedding* (Ron Bass)
- *My Big Fat Greek Wedding* (Nia Vardalos)
- *Napoleon Dynamite* (Jared Hess and Jerusha Hess)
- *Network* (Paddy Chayefsky)
- *Nurse Betty* (John C. Richards and James Flamberg)
- *The People vs. Larry Flynt* (Scott Alexander and Larry Karaszewski)
- *Philadelphia* (Ron Nyswaner)
- *Pi* (Darren Aronofsky, Sean Gullette, and Eric Watson)
- *Pitch Perfect* (Kay Cannon)
- *Planes, Trains, and Automobiles* (John Hughes)
- *The Professional* (Jacques Audiard, Michel Audiard, and Georges Lautner)
- *Pulp Fiction* (Quentin Tarantino)
- *Raiders of the Lost Ark* (Lawrence Kasdan)
- *School of Rock* (Mike White)
- *The Sea Inside* (Alejandro Amenábar and Mateo Gil)
- *Secrets and Lies* (Mike Leigh)
- *Se7en* (Andrew Kevin Walker)
- *Shakespeare in Love* (Marc Norman and Tom Stoppard)
- *Shall We Kiss?* (Emmanuel Mouret)
- *Shine* (Jan Sardi)
- *The Shining* (Stanley Kubrick and Diane Johnson)
- *Sin City* (Frank Miller and Robert Rodriguez)
- *The Sixth Sense* (M. Night Shyamalan)
- *Sliding Doors* (Peter Howitt)
- *Snatch* (Guy Ritchie)
- *The Spanish Prisoner* (David Mamet)
- *Spotlight* (Josh Singer, Tom McCarthy)
- *The Sting* (David S. Ward)

- *Summer of Sam* (Spike Lee, Victor Colicchio, and Michael Imperioli)
- *Sunset Boulevard* (Charles Brackett, Billy Wilder, and D.M. Marshman Jr.)
- *Superbad* (Seth Rogen, Evan Goldberg)
- *Tender Mercies* (Horton Foote)
- *The Terminator* (James Cameron and Gale Anne Hurd)
- *Thelma & Louise* (Callie Khouri)
- *Tie Me Up! Tie Me Down!* (Pedro Almodóvar)
- *Titanic* (James Cameron)
- *Tootsie* (Larry Gelbart and Murray Schisgal)
- *The Truman Show* (Andrew Niccol)
- *The Usual Suspects* (Christopher McQuarrie)
- *On the Waterfront* (Budd Schulberg)
- *Women on the Verge of a Nervous Breakdown* (Pedro Almodóvar)
- *You Can Count on Me* (Kenneth Lonergan)
- *Zootopia* (Jared Bush, Byron Howard, Rich Moore, Jim Reardon, Josie Trinidad, Phil Johnston, and Jennifer Lee)

OUR FAVORITE ADAPTATION SCREENPLAYS

An adaptation is creating a screenplay or series bible from an existing literary property.

- *A Few Good Men* (Aaron Sorkin, based on his play)
- *A Time to Kill* (Akiva Goldsman, from novel by John Grisham)
- *About a Boy* (Peter Hedges, Chris Weitz, and Paul Weitz, from novel by Nick Hornby)
- *About Last Night* (Tim Kazurinsky, from David Mamet's play *Sexual Perversity in Chicago*)
- *The Accidental Tourist* (Frank Galati and Lawrence Kasden, from novel by Anne Tyler)
- *Amadeus* (Peter Schaffer, based on his play)
- *Babe* (George Miller and Chris Noonan, from novel *The Sheep-Pig* by Dick King-Smith)
- *Batman Begins* (Christopher Nolan and David S. Goyer, based on characters from DC Comics)
- *Behind Enemy Lines* (David Veloz and Zak Penn, from story by Jim Thomas and John Thomas)
- *Being There* (Jerzy Kosińksi, based on his novel)
- *The Big Short* (Adam McKay and Charles Randolph, from book by Michael Lewis)
- *Bride and Prejudice* (Sanaa Hamri, from *Pride and Prejudice* by Jane Austen)
- *Closely Watched Trains* (Bohumil Hrabal and Jiří Menzel, based on Bohumil Hrabal's book)

- *Coal Miner's Daughter* (Tom Riekmann, from book by Loretta Lynn and George Vecsey)
- *The Color of Money* (Richard Price, from novel by Walter Tevis)
- *Contact* (James V. Hart, Michael Goldenberg, from novel by Carl Sagan, from story by Ann Druyan)
- *The Counterfeiters* (Stefan Ruzowitzky, based on *Die Fälscher* by Adolf Burger)
- *Dangerous Liaisons* (Christopher Hampton, based on his play *Les Liaisons Dangereuses*, from novel by Pierre Choderlos)
- *Fatal Attraction* (James Dearden, based on his teleplay, *Diversion*)
- *The Fault in Our Stars* (Scott Neustadter, Michael H. Weber, from novel by John Green)
- *Field of Dreams* (Philip Alden Robinson, from novel *Shoeless Joe* by W. P. Kinsella)
- *Fight Club* (Jim Uhls, from novel by Chuck Palahniuk)
- *Forrest Gump* (Eric Roth, from novel by Winston Groom)
- *The Fugitive* (David Twohy and Jeb Stuart, from TV series by Roy Higgins)
- *The Godfather* (Mario Puzo and Francis Ford Coppola, from novel by Mario Puzo)
- *Gone with the Wind* (Sidney Howard, from novel by Margaret Mitchell)
- *The Graduate* (Calder Willingham and Buck Henry, from novel by Charles Webb)
- *The Horse Whisperer* (Eric Roth and Richard LaGravenese, from novel by Nicholas Evans)
- *Il Postino* (Anna Pavignano, Michael Radford, Furio Scarpelli, Giacomo Scarpelli, and Massimo Troisi, from novel *Ardiente Paciencia* by Antonio Skármeta)

- *Inside Moves* (Valerie Curtin and Barry Levinson, from book by Todd Walton)
- *Jaws* (Peter Benchley and Carl Gottlieb, based on Benchley's novel)
- *To Kill a Mockingbird* (Horton Foote, from novel by Harper Lee)
- *The Kite Runner* (David Benioff, from novel by Khaled Hosseini)
- *Kramer vs. Kramer* (Robert Benton, from novel by Avery Corman)
- *Lawrence of Arabia* (Robert Bolt and Michael Wilson, based on *Seven Pillars of Wisdom* by T. E. Lawrence)
- *Layer Cake* (J.J. Connolly, based on his novel)
- *Leaving Las Vegas* (Mike Figgis, from novel by John O'Brien)
- *Legally Blonde* (Karen McCullah and Kirsten Smith, from novel by Amanda Brown)
- *Lion* (Saroo Brierley and Luke Davies, from book by Saroo Brierley with Larry Buttrose)
- *Live Flesh* (Pedro Almodóvar, Jorge Guerricaechevarría, and Ray Loriga, from a psychological thriller by Ruth Rendell) *Men in Black* (Ed Solomon, adapted from *The Men in Black* comic book series created by Lowell Cunningham and Sandy Carruthers)
- *Midnight Cowboy* (Waldo Salt, from novel by James Leo Herlihy)
- *Moneyball* (Aaron Sorkin, from novel by Michael Lewis)
- *My Life as a Dog* (Lasse Hallström, Brasse Brännström, Per Berglund from novel by Reidar Jönsson)
- *Notes on a Scandal* (Patrick Marber, from novel by Zoë Heller)
- *The Odd Couple* (Neil Simon, based on his play)
- *On Golden Pond* (Ernest Thompson, based on his novel)
- *One Flew Over the Cuckoo's Nest* (Lawrence Hauben and Bo Goldman, from novel by Ken Kesey)
- *Ordinary People* (Alvin Sargent, from novel by Judith Guest)

- *Out of Africa* (Kurt Luedtke, from memoir by Isak Dinesen)
- *Patton* (Francis Ford Coppola and Edmund H. North, based on the biography *Patton: Ordeal and Triumph* by Ladislas Farago and the memoir *A Soldier's Story* by Omar Bradley)
- *Perfume* (Andrew Birkin, Bernd Eichinger, Tom Tykwer, from novel by Patrick Süskind)
- *The Pianist* (Ronald Harwood based on the autobiography by Władysław Szpilman)
- *Postcards from the Edge* (Carrie Fisher, based on her semi-autobiographical book)
- *Pride and Prejudice* (Paul Mayeda Berges and Gurinder Chadha, from novel by Jane Austen)
- *Primal Fear* (Steve Shagan and Ann Biderman, from novel by William Diehl)
- *The Prince of Tides* (Becky Johnston and Pat Conroy, based on Conroy's novel)
- *Psycho* (Joseph Stefano, from novel by Robert Bloch)
- *Same Time, Next Year* (Bernard Slade, based on his play)
- *The Shawshank Redemption* (Frank Darabont, from short story "Rita Hayworth and the Shawshank Redemption" by Stephen King)
- *Sideways* (Alexander Payne and Jim Taylor, from novel by Rex Pickett)
- *The Silence of the Lambs* (Ted Tally, from novel by Thomas Harris)
- *Silver Linings Playbook* (David O. Russell, from book by Matthew Quick)
- *Sling Blade* (Billy Bob Thornton, based on his short film, *Some Folks Call It a Sling Blade)*
- *The Social Network* (Aaron Sorkin, adapted from *The Accidental Billionaires* by Ben Mezrich)

161

- *Slumdog Millionaire* (Simon Beaufoy, from novel *Q & A* by Vikas Swarup)
- *Sophie's Choice* (Alan J. Pakula, from book by William Styron)
- *Some Like It Hot* (Billy Wilder and I.A.L. Diamond, suggested by Robert Thoeren and Michael Logan)
- *Stand by Me* (Raynold Gideon and Bruce A. Evans, from novella *The Body* by Stephen King)
- *Terms of Endearment* (James L. Brooks, from novel by Larry McMurtry)
- *Three Kings* (David O. Russell, based on a story by John Ridley)
- *Trainspotting* (John Hodge, based on novel by Irvine Walsh)
- *Up in the Air* (Jason Reitman and Sheldon Turner, from book by Walter Kim)
- *Whiplash* (Damien Chazelle, based on his short film)
- *The Wings of the Dove* (Hossein Amini, from novel by Henry James)
- *Wonder Boys* (Steve Kloves, from novel by Steven Chabon)
- *Wonder Woman* (Allan Heinberg, Zack Snyder, Jason Fuchs, from comic by William Moulton Marston)
- *The Year of Living Dangerously* (David Williamson, Peter Weir, from novel by Christopher Koch)

OUR FAVORITE DRAMA SERIES

- *24*
- *Billions*
- *Breaking Bad*
- *Boardwalk Empire*
- *Dawson's Creek*
- *Downton Abbey*
- *ER*
- *Felicity*
- *Friday Night Lights*
- *Game of Thrones*
- *The Good Wife*
- *Homeland*
- *House of Cards* (HBO)
- *How to Get Away with Murder*
- *Justified*
- *The Killing*
- *Killing Eve*
- *Mad Men*
- *Masters of Sex*
- *Madame Secretary*
- *Mozart in the Jungle*
- *NYPD Blue*
- *Once and Again*
- *Ozark*
- *Queen Sugar*

- *Orange Is the New Black*
- *Orphan Black*
- *Outlander*
- *Queer as Folk*
- *Ray Donovan*
- *Reign*
- *Revenge*
- *Scandal*
- *Six Feet Under*
- *The Sopranos*
- *Stranger Things*
- *Thirteen Reasons Why*
- *This Is Us*
- *The Tudors*
- *The Twilight Zone*
- *West Wing*
- *The Wire*
- *The Wonder Years*

OUR FAVORITE COMEDY SERIES

- *30 Rock*
- *Absolutely Fabulous*
- *Arrested Development*
- *Black-ish* (ABC)
- *Brooklyn 99*
- *Cheers*
- *Curb Your Enthusiasm*
- *Gilmore Girls (comedy-drama)*
- *Entourage*
- *Everybody Loves Raymond*
- *Friends*
- *The Golden Girls*
- *I Love Lucy*
- *The Larry Sanders Show*
- *Life in Pieces*
- *The Marvelous Mrs. Maisel*
- *Master of None*
- *Modern Family* (ABC)
- *The Office* (The British and American versions)
- *Saturday Night Live*
- *Seinfeld*
- *The Simpsons*
- *Trial & Error*
- *Unbreakable Kimmy Schmidt* (Netflix)
- *Veep* (HBO)
- *Will & Grace*

OUR FAVORITE LIMITED SERIES

- *American Crime*
- *Band of Brothers*
- *Big Little Lies* (HBO)
- *The Crown* (Netflix)
- *Fargo*
- *Genius* (NatGeo)
- *Lonesome Dove*
- *Roots (1977)*
- *Victoria*

OUR FAVORITE STORIES ABOUT STORYTELLING

- *The Odyssey,* Homer
- *One Thousand and One Nights,* Translated by Richard Francis Burton
- *The Decameron,* Giovanni Boccaccio
- *The Canterbury Tales,* Geoffrey Chaucer
- *Don Quixote de la Mancha,* Miguel de Cervantes
- *The Life and Opinions of Tristram Shandy, Gentleman,* Laurence Sterne
- *One Hundred Years of Solitude,* Gabriel García Márquez
- *A Palpable God,* Reynolds Price
- *The Shadow of the Wind,* Carlos Ruiz Zafrón

CONTEMPORARY NOVELISTS WHO'VE EARNED THE MOST

"Show me the money!"

—*Jerry Maguire*

This list is a moving target, but the writers listed here alphabetically have all made multimillions from their respective works (representative title in parentheses). It'd be a great idea, should you wish to count yourself among them, to buy or borrow their books and read them. We hope this allays any doubt that it can't be done!

- Maeve Binchy (*Circle of Friends*)
- Barbara Taylor Bradford (*A Woman of Substance*)
- Dan Brown (*The Da Vinci Code*)
- Agatha Christie (*And Then There Were None*)
- Mary Higgins Clark (*The Shadow of Your Smile*)
- James Clavell (*Shōgun*)
- Tom Clancy (*The Hunt for Red October*)
- Paul Coelho (*The Alchemist*)
- Jackie Collins (*Hollywood Wives*)
- Robin Cook (*Coma*)
- Michael Crichton (*Jurassic Park*)
- Clive Cussler (*The Sea Hunters*)
- Dominick Dunne (*The Two Mrs. Grenvilles*)
- James Ellroy (*L.A. Confidential*)
- Janet Evanovich (*Sizzling Sixteen*)
- Ian Fleming (*Casino Royale*)
- Ken Follett (*Eye of the Needle*)

- Sue Grafton (*The Alphabet Mysteries*)
- John Grisham (*The Firm*)
- E. L. James (*Fifty Shades of Grey*)
- Jonathan Kellerman (*When the Bough Breaks*)
- Stephen King (*The Shining*)
- Dean Koontz (*Demon Child*)
- Judith Krantz (*Scruples*)
- Tim LaHaye and Jerry B. Jenkins (*Left Behind* Series)
- Stieg Larsson (*The Girl with the Dragon Tattoo*)
- Astrid Lindgren (*Pipi Longstocking*)
- Robert Ludlum (*The Bourne Identity*)
- George R. R. Martin (*A Song of Fire and Ice*, which became *Game of Thrones*)
- Alistair McLean (*The Guns of Navarone*)
- Stephenie Meyer (*Twilight* series)
- James Michener (*Hawaii*)
- Fern Michaels (*Déjà Vu*)
- James Patterson (*Kiss the Girls*)
- Rosamunde Pilcher (*Winter Solstice*)
- Anne Rice (*Interview with the Vampire*)
- Nora Roberts (*Chasing Fire*)
- Harold Robbins (*A Stone for Danny Fisher*)
- J. K. Rowling (the Harry Potter series)
- Sidney Sheldon (*Master of the Game*)
- Nicholas Sparks (*The Notebook*)
- Danielle Steel (*A Good Woman*)
- R. L. Stine (the *Goosebumps* series)
- Scott Turow (*Presumed Innocent*)
- John Updike (*Rabbit, Run*)

HIGHEST-PAID SCREENWRITERS

"Not every story has explosions and car chases. That's why they have nudity and espionage."

—Bill Barnes and Gene Ambaum

This list is also a moving target, but the screenwriters listed here alphabetically have all made multimillions from their work in Hollywood. Should you aspire to be counted among them, download their scripts from www.sfy.ru and study every one of them. Each entry shows only one representative title.

- David Ayer (*The Fast and the Furious*)
- Ron Bass (*Rain Man*)
- David Benioff (*The Kite Runner*)
- Shane Black (*Lethal Weapon*)
- James Cameron (*Avatar*)
- William Davies (*Twins*)
- Gerald DiPego (*Message in a Bottle*)
- Leslie Dixon (*Mrs. Doubtfire*)
- Nora Ephron (*Sleepless in Seattle*)
- Patrick Sheane Duncan (*Courage Under Fire*)
- Joe Eszterhas (*Basic Instinct*)
- Peter Jackson (*King Kong*)
- Laeta Kalogridis (*Terminator Genisys*)
- David Koepp (*Spiderman*)
- Dale Launer (*My Cousin Vinny*)

- Jennifer Lee (*Frozen*)
- Irene Mecchi (*The Hunchback of Notre Dame*)
- Nancy Meyers (*What Women Want*)
- Melissa Rosenberg (*Twilight*)
- Scott Rosenberg (*Con Air*)
- Lana Wachowski (*The Matrix*)
- Randall Wallace (*Braveheart*)
- Linda Woolverton (*Maleficent*)
- M. Night Shyamalan (*The Sixth Sense*)
- Amanda Silver (*Jurassic World*).
- Akiva Goldsman (*Angels & Demons*)

Londoner **Adam Croft** published his ninth book, *Her Last Tomorrow*, at age twenty-nine. Through tenacious Facebook marketing, he reached the one-million mark in sales by the end of 2016. Amazon's imprint, Thomas & Mercer, took notice and struck a deal with Croft. Eighty percent of Croft's sales came from Kindle sales. Croft wasn't shooting for the stars with this release. He'd been disappointed with sales in the past—eight times to be exact. Now, he's making over $2,000 a day.

APPENDIX A:
Exemplary Marketing Plan

Failure to Freedom by Jeffrey Tanenhaus

PLATFORM & PRESS

The strength of my platform is **expertise** that combines authenticity and accomplishment.

Connections in my corner right now include successful bloggers, authors, media contacts, and cycling community influencers. My engaging **personality** and **presentation skills** are assets, too. My human-interest story captured the attention of traditional and digital media. **Previous press** proves that my message is meaningful, and my journey is deeper than a one-dimensional bike trip.

Expertise

- I'm authentic and credible. No corporate sponsors. No support team. Just me against the world.
- I'm relatable. 3,000,000 people quit their jobs every month. 100,000 New Yorkers and 34,000 Chicagoans ride bike share as annual members. People dislike work but love to bike!
- The message resonates. People look for inspiration and happiness in life. I survived a trial by ordeal and share motivational nuggets of wisdom to self-empower others.
- Recognition. People don't know my name, but they recall two salient facts: a guy rode a Citi Bike cross-country and a guy on a Citi Bike got beat up in Oklahoma.

Connections are an email or call away

• Travel and lifestyle bloggers (and personal friends) with loyal Millennial followers on Facebook: Nomadic Matt 182,000 | Lee Abbamonte 115,000 | Adventurous Kate 54,000 | TravelFreak 15,000

• Authors (and personal friends) of travel books: Amanda Pressner, co-author *The Lost Girls*

(Harper Perennial) | Matt Gross, author *The Turk Who Loved Apples* (Da Capo Press), editor

BonAppetit.com and former *NYT* Frugal Traveler | Jason Cochran, Editor-in-Chief Frommers.com

• Leadership of advocacy groups: NYC Transportation Alternatives 150,000 members |

Bike Pittsburgh 23,100 on email list | LA County Bike Coalition 10,000 on email list

• Heads of organizations: Adventure Cycling 50,000 members | warmshowers.org cyclist Facebook group 24,000 members | Assn. of Pedestrian & Bicycle Professionals 1,300 members

• Cousin of Sam Tanenhaus, former editor of *The New York Times Book Review*

• Editors of trade magazines: *Bicycling* | *Bicycle Times* | *MomentumMag*

• *Dartmouth Alumni Magazine* 58,800 paid/requested circulation, including 1,100 from my graduating class for which I'm the newsletter's co-editor

• 4,000 active monthly users of my iPhone/iPad app *New York City Essential Guide*

• Any influencer in Tulsa (metro pop. 981,000) and all TV/print/literary media, 1° of separation

Social media

• Authenticity is my guiding principle. I don't pay for followers or use software bots to artificially inflate my metrics, which is sadly widespread nowadays.

• My preferred channel is Instagram, now a more influential platform than Twitter. My following is a modest 1,500, but engagement (likes + comments / followers) is a robust 9.5% to 14% for top performing posts and 6.6% per average post—double that of major brands—3.3% engagement per post for top 25 engaging brands on Instagram, as per Business Insider-Socialbakers 2014 study.

Personality & Presentation

• Engaging public speaker with multimedia skills;
humorous, down-to-earth, likable

• Guest on *The Late Show with Stephen Colbert*

• Paid to contribute to Mashable and Elite Daily; Mashable article peaked at #1 in "hot"

• Special guest speaker at a congressional fundraiser for a bike-friendly representative from Oregon

• Invited to speak at New York Travel Festival and WE-cycle bike film festival in Aspen, Colorado

• Bike is most photographed item at Tulsa Historical Society's transportation exhibit, *On the Move*

PROMOTION IDEAS

Marketing strategy to be developed by the editor and publishing house. Author's initial ideas include:

Book trailer

- Splice photos, videos with TV/radio coverage into a professionally produced, high-impact trailer

Strategic reviews

- Reach out to top reviewers of similar topics on goodreads.com and amazon.com with advance reading copy to seed reviews and boost discoverability of book upon launch
- Reward most loyal social media followers with advance reading copy and personal message

Network outreach

- Write guest posts for influential travel bloggers (and personal friends) with 100,000+ Millennial followers: nomadicmatt.com, leeabbamote.com, adventerouskate.com, travelfreak.net
- Tap "big mouth" friends with strong PR reach to connect me with their relevant media contacts
- Mobilize contacts in the bicycle industry, advocacy community, and media

Author events

- Cross-promotional events with bicycle or travel groups, including bike share programs
- Book tour with readings at bookstores and bicycle shops, including cities I biked through
- Conference and motivational speaker
- Leverage my forthcoming bike hostel venture in Tulsa to promote book
- Include book with permanent exhibition of bike at Tulsa's Route 66 Museum (opening 2018)

APPENDIX B:
Generic Option-Purchase Agreement

As of August ____, _____

_____

_____

_____

Dear Messrs. _____ and _____:

This will confirm the agreement between _____ ("Purchaser") and both of you (collectively "you") with respect to the original, unpublished, unexploited screenplay entitled "_____" written by you (which, together with the title, themes, contents and characters, and all translations, adaptations, and other versions thereof now or hereafter owned by you, whether now existing or hereafter created, is hereinafter called the "Property").

In consideration of the parties' mutual promises, it is hereby agreed as follows:

1. OPTION

(a) You hereby exclusively and irrevocably grant to Purchaser two (2) consecutive options (the "Option"), each lasting for one (1) year, to purchase all rights in the Property as set forth in Paragraph 6 hereof (the "Rights"). The initial option period shall commence on the date on which you deliver this Agreement and all attachments hereto to Purchaser fully-executed. The initial option period may be extended by Purchaser for the second option period at any time prior to the expiration of the initial option period.

(b) The initial option period shall be at a cost of Two Thousand Five Hundred Dollars ($2,500), payable upon the full execution hereof. The second option period shall be at a cost of Two Thousand Dollars ($2,000), payable, if at all, not later than the expiration of the initial option period. The option payment with respect to the initial option period shall be applicable against the Purchase Price (as defined below). The option payment with respect to the second option period shall not apply against said Purchase Price.

(c) During the option period (and extensions thereof, if any), Purchaser shall have the right to engage in or arrange for preproduction with respect to motion pictures and/or other productions intended to be based on the Property. The first such motion picture or other production is referred to herein as the "Picture." If in connection with such preproduction another party is engaged by Purchaser to write screenplays or other materials based on the Property, all such writings shall be and remain Purchaser's sole and exclusive property (whether or not Purchaser exercises the Option hereunder).

2.   PURCHASE PRICE. If Purchaser exercises the Option, the purchase price for the Rights shall be the following amount ("Purchase Price"), as applicable:

(a) Self-Financing or Co-Financing. If Purchaser self-finances or co-finances the Picture with a third party, Twenty Thousand Dollars ($20,000), less the initial option payment. In the event Purchaser co-finances the Picture with a third party (as opposed to an outright sale or self-financing), then, depending upon the amount of the budget of the Picture, Purchaser agrees to use reasonable efforts to increase the Purchase Price. In the event Purchaser enters into a binding unconditional agreement with a third party pursuant to which such third party acquires outright all rights in and to the Property, then you shall be entitled to receive the greater of said Twenty Thousand

Dollars ($20,000) or one-third (1/3) of the net profits generated from such sale. For purposes of this Paragraph 2(a) only, "net profits" shall be determined as follows: all gross amounts actually received by Purchaser from the sale of all rights in the Property, less the following deductions: (i) Purchaser's actual out-of-pocket costs incurred in connection with developing and producing the Picture; plus (ii) an overhead charge in an amount equal to fifteen percent (15%) of (i) plus interest on (i), and (ii) at the prime rate charged by the Bank of America (Los Angeles Branch) at the time, plus two percent (2%).

(b) Third Party Financing. If a studio or other third party fully finances the Picture, in lieu of the amount set forth in (a), an amount equal to two and one-half percent (2-1/2%) of the final approved budget of the Picture, less the initial option payment, up to a maximum ceiling of Two Hundred and Fifty Thousand Dollars ($250,000). The "final approved budget" shall be the going-in budget of the Picture, exclusive of interest, financing charges, completion bond fees, overhead and any contingency.

(c) Exercise Date. The Option, if exercised, shall be exercised by written notice or by commencement of principal photography of the Picture, whichever is sooner.

3. NET PROFITS

If the Option is exercised and the Picture is produced and released based on the Rights granted and material written by you hereunder, and if pursuant to a final credit determination under this Agreement you shall receive screenplay credit in connection with the Picture, provided that Purchaser does not sell outright the rights to produce the Picture to a third party, Purchaser will pay you:

(a) If you receive sole "screenplay by" or sole "written by" credit ("Sole Credit"), an amount equal to five percent (5%) of one hundred percent (100%) of the Net Profits of the Picture; and

(b) If you receive shared "screenplay by" or shared "written by" credit with any other writer or writers ("Shared Credit"), an amount equal to two and one-half percent (2–1/2%) of one hundred percent (100%) of the Net Profits of the Picture.

(c) In the event Purchaser solely finances the Picture, Purchaser shall have the right to, in lieu of the amounts set forth in subparagraph (a) or (b) above, elect to pay you either (i) five percent (5%) of Purchaser's Net Profits or (ii) five percent (5%) of the first $100,000 of Net Profits received by Purchaser, plus seven and one-half percent (7.5%) of the second $100,000 of Net Profits received by Purchaser, plus ten percent (10%) of the next Three Hundred Thousand Dollars ($300,000) of Net Profits received by Purchaser, and fifteen percent (15%) of the Net Profits received by Purchaser in excess of Five Hundred Thousand Dollars ($500,000). Purchaser's election under this paragraph shall be made prior to the date of commencement of principal photography.

The "Net Profits" referred to in this Agreement shall be computed, determined and payable in accordance with and subject to the definition of net profits applicable to Purchaser in its agreement with the distributor of the Picture, if there is one worldwide distributor of the Picture which provides the entire financing for the Picture, and if there is more than one distributor and/or the single worldwide distributor does not provide the entire financing for the Picture, then in accordance with Purchaser's standard definition of net profits, which shall in any event provide for, without limitation, recoupment of all of Purchaser's costs in connection with the Picture, interest and overhead of 15%. Included in the cost of production shall be a producer's fee to Purchaser in an amount not to exceed Two Hundred Thousand Dollars ($200,000). The definition of Net Profits accorded to you pursuant to this Paragraph 3 shall in any event be no less favorable than the definition accorded any third party.

4. "PASSIVE" PAYMENTS

(a) If the Picture, as released, was based on the rights granted and material written by you hereunder and if you shall receive sole writing credit in connection therewith, and provided you shall faithfully and completely keep and perform each and every covenant and condition of this Agreement on your part to be kept and performed, then for a period of five (5) years after the initial release of the Picture, if Purchaser elects, in its sole discretion, to produce or authorize the production of the initial theatrical sequel, initial theatrical remake, MOW, miniseries or TV series pilot based upon the Picture, and if you do not render writing services in connection with such theatrical remake, theatrical sequel, MOW, miniseries or TV pilot, then you shall be entitled to receive the following passive payments (reduced by one-half (1/2) for shared credit.

(i) Additional Payments: Sequel or Remake Theatrical Motion Pictures

(1) For each sequel motion picture intended for initial theatrical release which is produced by or under the authority of Purchaser and which is based upon the Picture, you shall be paid an amount equal to one half (1/2) of the sums actually paid to you under Paragraph 2 hereof, plus an amount equal to one half (1/2) of the applicable percentage (if any) specified in Paragraph 3 hereof, of the Net Profits of such sequel.

(2) For each remake motion picture intended for initial theatrical release which is produced by or under the authority of Purchaser and which is based upon the Picture, you shall be paid an amount equal to one third (1/3) of the sums actually paid to you for the Picture under Paragraph 2, plus an amount equal to one third (1/3) of the

applicable percentage (if any) specified in Paragraph 3 hereof, of the Net Profits of such remake.

(3) The fixed sums due you pursuant to this subparagraph (i) shall be payable upon commencement of principal photography of such sequel or remake theatrical motion picture, as the case may be.

(4) The foregoing payments for sequel or remake theatrical motion pictures shall entitle Purchaser to unlimited rights of exhibition and exploitation with respect to each such sequel or remake in perpetuity, in any and all media whether now existing or hereafter devised.

(ii) Additional Payments Television Series

For each production produced by or under the authority of Purchaser which is an episode of a television series, and which series is based upon the Picture, and which is intended for initial exhibition on free United States prime time network television, you shall be paid the following amounts (reducible by one-half (1/2) for episodes intended for initial exhibition in the United States on other than free prime-time network television), such payment for each such episode shall be made upon the broadcast of each such episode:

(1) One Thousand Two Hundred Fifty Dollars ($1,250) for each episode of not more than thirty (30) minutes in length.

(2) One Thousand Five Hundred Dollars ($1,500) for each episode of more than thirty (30) minutes but not more than sixty (60) minutes in length; and

(3) One Thousand Seven Hundred Fifty Dollars ($1,750) for each episode of more than sixty (60) minutes in length; and

(4) If any such television program is rerun, you shall be paid one hundred percent (100%) of the applicable sum initially paid you pursuant to subparagraphs (ii) (1) through (ii) (3) above spread over the second, third, fourth, fifth, and sixth runs. No further rerun payments shall be due or payable for any run after the sixth run.

(iii) Additional Payments MOW or Mini-Series

For each motion picture produced by or under the authority of Purchaser which is an MOW or miniseries, and which is based upon the Picture, and which is intended for initial exhibition in the United States on free prime time network television, you shall be paid Ten Thousand Dollars ($10,000) for each hour thereof, up to a maximum of Eighty Thousand Dollars ($80,000), reducible by one-half (1/2) if intended for initial exhibition in the United States on other than free prime-time network television. Such payment shall be made upon broadcast of the MOW or Mini-Series.

(iv) Application of Payments

The amounts payable to you under this Paragraph 4 shall be deemed an advance against and deductible from (or where allowed, in lieu of) any amounts which may become payable to you pursuant to the Writers Guild of America ("WGA") Basic Agreement ("WGA Agreement") or any other guild agreement which may be applicable, in connection with television programs, sequel or remake theatrical motion pictures, and the reverse shall also be the case. No duplication of payment or second payment under this Paragraph 4 shall be made to you in the event that the theatrical sequel or remake shall be released for television exhibition or in the event that any television program, sequel or remake shall be released theatrically.

5.   Writing Services. In consideration for the amounts payable to you hereunder, and other good and valuable consideration, the receipt and adequacy of which you hereby acknowledge, you shall perform such rewrite and polish services as may be required by Purchaser in connection with the Property from the date hereof until completion of principal photography of the Picture, if any. No additional sums shall be payable to you in connection with the writing services which may be required by Purchaser pursuant to this paragraph. All results and proceeds of your writing services

hereunder are being performed for Purchaser as a work-made-for-hire, with Purchaser being deemed the sole author and copyright holder thereof throughout the universe in perpetuity.

6. RIGHTS.

(a) If the Option is exercised, you hereby assign to Purchaser, exclusively, in perpetuity and throughout the universe, all right, title and interest, including the entire copyright, in the Property, including, without limitation, all motion picture rights, all television rights (pay, free, film, tape, cassette, cable, live and otherwise) and all allied and incidental rights in the Property, including, by way of further illustration, sequel and remake rights, music rights, soundtrack album rights, merchandising rights, radio rights, stage rights and promotional and advertising rights.

(b) The rights herein granted include the right to distribute, transmit, exhibit, broadcast and otherwise exploit all works produced pursuant to the rights granted hereunder by means of any and all media and devices whether now known or hereafter devised, and in any and all markets whatsoever, as well as the right of Purchaser in its discretion to make any and all changes in, additions to and deletions from the Property, as well as the right to use, in a reasonable and customary manner, your name, likeness and biography in and in connection with the exploitation of the rights granted hereunder; provided, that in no event shall your name, likeness and/or biography be used hereunder to endorse any product, service, individual or entity, or other than in connection with the exploitation of the rights granted hereunder. Nothing contained in this Option Agreement shall be construed as requiring Purchaser to exercise or exploit any of the rights granted to Purchaser hereunder.

(c) You agree that Purchaser shall have the unlimited right to vary, change, alter, modify, add to and/or delete from all or any part of the Property (including without limitation the title or titles thereto), and to rearrange and/or transpose all or any part of the Property and change the sequence thereof and the characters and descriptions of the characters contained in the Property and to use a portion or portions of the Property in conjunction with any other literary, dramatic or other material of any kind.

7. REPRESENTATIONS AND WARRANTIES

You hereby represent and warrant that: (a) the Property and all material to be written by you hereunder (the "Revisions") is or shall be written by and shall be wholly original with you; (b) neither the Property, the Revisions nor any element thereof infringes the copyright in any other work; (c) neither the Property, the Revisions nor their exploitation will violate the rights to privacy or publicity of any person or constitute a defamation against any person, or in any other way violate the rights of any person whomsoever; (d) you own all rights optioned to Purchaser free and clear of any liens, encumbrances, and other third party interests, and any claims or litigation, whether pending or threatened; (e) you have full right and power to make and perform this Option Agreement without the consent of any third party; (f) the Property has not previously been exploited as a motion picture or television production; and (g) the Property does and will continue to enjoy either statutory or common law copyright protection in the United States and all countries adhering to either or both the Berne and Universal Copyright Conventions. You hereby agree to defend, indemnify and hold harmless Purchaser, its successors, licensees and assigns and the directors, shareholders, employees and agents of the foregoing, from and against any and all claims, damages, liabilities, costs and expenses (including reasonable attorneys' fees) arising out of the breach or alleged breach by you of any warranty or undertaking made or to be performed by you under the terms of this Option Agreement.

8. ADDITIONAL DOCUMENTS

At Purchaser's request and expense, you will execute any and all additional documents and instruments reasonably necessary or desirable to effectuate purposes of this Option Agreement (including, without limitation, short-form options and assignments in the form attached hereto and by this reference incorporated herein). You hereby irrevocably appoint Purchaser (or Purchaser's designee) as attorney-in-fact with full power to execute, acknowledge, deliver and record in the US Copyright Office or elsewhere any and all such documents which you fail to execute, acknowledge and deliver within five (5) business days after Purchaser's request therefor.

9. CREDIT

You shall receive screenplay credit on screen and in paid advertising issued by Purchaser or under its direct control in connection with the Picture as if the standards of the WGA Agreement controlled this Agreement (provided any decisions which under the WGA Agreement are to be made by the WGA or any arbitration panel shall instead be made by Purchaser in accordance with WGA standards). You shall also receive story credit on screen to be shared with _____ in size and position to be determined by Purchaser. In addition, you shall receive credit on screen as "co-producers" of the Picture in a size and position to be determined by Purchaser in its sole discretion. It is acknowledged and agreed that no casual or inadvertent failure by Purchaser to accord such credit nor the failure for any reason by third parties to comply with the pro-visions of this paragraph, shall be deemed a breach hereof by Purchaser. It is further acknowledged and agreed that neither such failure, nor any other breach of this Option Agreement, shall entitle you to equitable relief, whether injunctive or otherwise, against or with respect to the Picture or any other works produced pursuant to the rights granted hereunder or their exploitation, since your remedy of money damages at law is adequate.

10. COPYRIGHT

All rights granted and agreed to be granted to Purchaser under this Option Agreement shall be irrevocably vested in Purchaser (including, without limitation, for the full term of copyright protection everywhere in the world and any and all renewals thereof), and shall not be subject to rescission by you or any other party for any cause, nor shall said rights be subject to termination or **reversion** by operation of law or otherwise, except to the extent, if any, that the provisions of any copyright law or similar law relating to the right to terminate grants of, and/or recapture rights in, literary property may apply. If the rights granted to Purchaser hereunder shall revert to you pursuant to the provisions of any copyright law or similar law, and if you are at any time thereafter prepared to enter into an agreement with a third party for the license, exercise or other disposition of all or any of such rights, you shall, before entering into such agreement, give Purchaser written notice of the terms thereof and the party involved. Purchaser shall then have fourteen (14) days in which to elect to acquire the rights involved on the terms contained in the notice. If Purchaser so elects in writing, you shall enter into a written agreement with Purchaser with regard thereto.

11. FEDERAL COMMUNICATIONS ACT

You are aware that it is a criminal offense under the Federal Communications Act, as amended, for any person to accept or pay any money, service or other valuable consideration for the inclusion of any plug, reference, product identification or other matter as part of a television program, without disclosure in the manner required by law. You understand that it is the policy of Purchaser to prohibit the acceptance or payment of any such consideration, and you represent that you have not accepted or paid and agree that you shall not accept or pay any such consideration.

12. ASSIGNMENT

Purchaser shall have the right to assign any or all of its rights under this Option Agreement to any person, and any such assignment shall relieve Purchaser of its obligations to you under this Option Agreement, provided that such assignee assumes all of Purchaser's obligations hereunder in writing. You shall not have the right to assign this Option Agreement.

13. FORCE MAJEURE

The option period hereunder shall be subject to extension for any period of default and/or force majeure (including without limitation any strike by any guild, union or other labor organization against motion picture producers during the option period) if said force majeure event materially inhibits Purchaser's ability to develop the Property, and any period during which any claim remains outstanding or unresolved which involves the breach or alleged breach of any of your warranties, representations or agreements herein.

14. APPLICABLE LAW/JURISDICTION

This Agreement will be interpreted in accordance with the laws of the State of California applicable to agreements entered into and to be wholly performed therein. You hereby consent to the exclusive jurisdiction of the courts (State and Federal) located in the County of Los Angeles, State of California.

15. NOTICES

(a) All notices from Purchaser to you shall be sent to you at the address on page one hereof.

(b) All notices from you to Purchaser shall be sent to Purchaser at the address on page one hereof with a mandatory copy to:

_____

_____

_____

(c) All payments which Purchaser may be required to make to you hereunder shall be delivered or sent to you by mail or telegraph at the address for payments set forth on page one hereof, and you acknowledge that payment in such fashion shall be a good and valid discharge of all such indebtedness to you.

16. RENTAL RIGHT

You acknowledge and agree that the following sums are in consideration of, and constitute equitable remuneration for, the rental right included in the rights granted hereunder: (1) an agreed allocation to the rental right of 3.8% of the fixed compensation and, if applicable, 3.8% of the contingent compensation provided for in this Agreement; and (2) any sums payable to you with respect to the rental right under any applicable collective bargaining or other industry-wide agreement; and (3) the residuals payable to you under any such collective bargaining or industry-wide agreement with respect to home video exploitation which are reasonably attributable to sale of home video devices for rental purposes in the territories or jurisdictions where the rental right is recognized. If under the applicable law of any territory or jurisdiction, any additional or different form of compensation is required to satisfy the requirement of equitable remuneration, then it is agreed that the grant to Purchaser of the rental right shall nevertheless be fully effective, and Purchaser shall pay you such compensation or, if necessary, the parties shall in good faith negotiate the amount and nature thereof in accordance with applicable law. Since Purchaser has already paid or agreed to pay you equitable remuneration for the rental right, you hereby assign to Purchaser, except to the extent specifically reserved to you under any applicable collective bargaining or other industry-wide agreement, all compensation for the rental right payable or which may become payable to you on account or in the nature of a tax or levy, through a collecting society or otherwise. You shall cooperate fully with Purchaser in the collection and payment to Purchaser of such compensation. Further, since under this Agreement Purchaser has already paid or agreed to pay you full consideration for all rights granted by you hereunder, you hereby assign to Purchaser, except to the extent specifically reserved to you under any applicable collective bargaining or other industry-wide agreement, all other compensation payable or which may become payable to you on account or in the nature of a tax or levy, through a collecting society or otherwise, under the applicable law of any territory or jurisdiction, including by way of illustration only, so-called blank tape and similar levies. You shall cooperate fully with Purchaser in connection with the collection and payment to Purchaser of all such compensation.

17. IMMIGRATION REFORM ACT

You warrant and represent that you are eligible to be employed in the United States in compliance with the Immigration Reform Act of 1986, as amended. As a condition precedent to your receipt of any payment hereunder, you will complete the requisite I-9 Form and will present such form to Purchaser along with the requisite documentation, as specified on the I-9 Form, evidencing that you may be lawfully employed.

18. Conflict Waiver

The parties hereto acknowledge that the law firm of _____ ("Firm") has heretofore been retained by each of them as attorneys-at-law to furnish each of them legal advice and services, including with respect to the Property and this Agreement. The parties further acknowledge that, at their joint request, the Firm has drafted this letter agreement, which is intended to memorialize the agreement between the parties. We acknowledge that the Firm's joint representation of us has been with the knowledge, informed consent and approval of each of us, and we will not assert any claim at any time that the agreement is not valid because of such representation. We further acknowledge that we have been advised to seek, and have had ample opportunity to seek, independent business and legal counseling with respect to such representation and this Agreement.

19. ENTIRE UNDERSTANDING

This Agreement constitutes the entire understanding between the parties and cannot be modified except by written agreement signed by Purchaser and you.

20. MISCELLANEOUS

If there is any conflict between any provisions of this Option Agreement and any present or future statute, law, ordinance or regulation, the latter shall prevail; provided, that the provision hereof so affected shall be limited only to the extent necessary and no other provision shall be affected.

Please signify your agreement to the foregoing by signing this letter in the space provided below.

Very truly yours,

_____

By: _____

Its: _____

AGREED TO AND ACCEPTED:

Project Nephili

Based on the novel by T. L. Farmer

When a journalist researches a special interest story on a local mental hospital, she gets trapped in scandal involving the town's horrifying history of slavery, a lethal madman trying to stop it from being uncovered, an archaeological dig halfway across the world, and half-human beings who may be the key to tying everything together.

EPISODE 1: Blytheville, Georgia, 1938. A giant of a man flees for his life through dark woods. He's mulatto-skinned with long flowing locks. His piercing blue eyes reflect the moonlight.

He bursts out onto an open road. A truck speeding by clips him—he's dead before he hits the ground. The two white men driving leave to tell their boss, a Dr. Mede, what's happened. But meanwhile, a mysterious group of people who bear striking resemblance to the dead man emerge from the forest to say a silent prayer and take the body with them, evaporating into the mist.

Blytheville, Georgia, present day. Seasoned journalist ANGIE MCDOWELL (34) works at *The Blytheville Express* newspaper offices. She's recently been "released" from the *Atlanta Journal* due to excessive drinking.

Angie has just been given a special interest assignment by editor in chief EDGAR BLYTHE. Edgar's family roots run deep back to Blytheville's founding family, and that provides a power he's not afraid to flaunt. But in assigning this piece, it's clear that even he is under someone else's thumb...

Angie begrudgingly digs into the story: Blytheville State Hospital, institution for mental patients, has been under fire for years of bad management and abuse. Trying to establish a timeline, Angie looks into the hospital's past. It was once a plantation owned by BENJAMIN FRANKLIN BLYTHE, who sold it to the State of Georgia. It survived Sherman's March to become the hospital, adding wings for white, black, and mixed patients, and hiring many of the former plantation slaves to work in the lime quarry associated with the grounds.

Angie comes across a reference to a book titled *Come to Me You Who Labor and Are Heavy Laden: A History of South Central Asylum for the Insane*, published in 1967 by RUTHERFORD HOFFMANN, chaplain at the asylum for twenty-five years. The book speaks of mistreatment of African American patients during his tenure at the hospital. But there are no copies available for purchase anywhere, and the local library hasn't seen their copy in years. Hoffmann has since passed. It's seemingly a dead end.

When Angie leaves the office that night, she has an eerie feeling she's being followed. She makes it to her car and manages to drive off.

But her would-be assailant, BUDDY ZANE, isn't so lucky. He's ambushed in his attempt to get to Angie, then run off the road and killed by a mysterious driver in a black Lincoln Navigator.

Arriving home, Angie discovers a piece of paper nailed to her door with a strange elliptical symbol on it. She emails a photo of the paper to BLAKE CHILDS (30s), a former colleague and brief fling who now works as a pathologist and field agent for the Georgia Bureau of Investigation (GBI).

The next day, Angie visits the hospital. She's greeted by FLO DOBSON (97), a former nurse who now gives weekly tours of the grounds. Flo is insensitive, seemingly stuck in the vernacular of the 60s. She also looks incredibly youthful for her 97 years. As they walk through the Hospital, Angie makes note of a portrait of plantation owner Blythe in which he's clutching a copy of Darwin's *The Origin of Species*.

Flo allows Angie to explore the grounds on her own, and while out by the now-unused slaves' quarters Angie senses a strange energy around her. She's spooked by a figure in white floating across the darkness, causing her to trip and fall and hit her head on a metal stake in the ground. The stake is labeled: 98342.

When Angie questions her about it, Flo claims the stakes are just old surveyor's markers from laying out plans for the building. She seems to have a well-though-out answer for everything.

Flo takes care of Angie's minor injuries in Dr. Mede's old office, the man who founded and ran the hospital in its heyday. Angie scans the books on his shelf, finding an old and well-worn copy of Darwin. She sees that a chapter on "Hybridism" is bookmarked. Her question now: How are Dr. Mede and Captain Franklin Blythe, the former plantation owner, connected?

The next day, Agent Blake Childs comes to see Angie. The connection between them is rekindled. The GBI is buzzing over the paper that was nailed to her door—analysis tells them the paper itself is over 300 years old, but they can't figure out what the language is, even though one of their linguists claims it has similarities to the ancient Dogon Tribes of West Africa. Angie can't imagine why the paper was nailed to her door.

Angie gets in touch with unofficial town historian REVEREND SHELDON MASTERSON in hopes of finding out more about Hoffmann's apparently missing book. Masterson is clearly on edge and frustrated during their meeting, point-blank telling Angie that her digging may get her into trouble.

Suspicions raised, she follows him after their meeting. He first stops at a bank, where he leaves with a wrapped object, then follows him to the state hospital, where he leaves without the object. But there's nothing Angie can do about it now except make note in her notebook.

Following her meeting with Masterson, Edgar Blythe pulls Angie off the hospital story because "she's pissing too many people off." Once again, he seems to be operating under someone else's thumb, and this leaves Angie furious. She heads home to pass out in a drunken rage, falling into a dark space reminiscent of hard times in her life. She dreams of immensely tall men and women with mulatto skin, long dreadlocks, bright blue eyes, and six fingers on each hand. They're gentle, kind, and almost ethereal, urging her to keep moving forward, to not give up on the story. The seeming leader of these people introduces herself as SALLIE. The symbol Angie found on her door replays in the dream over and over.

EPISODE 2: Atlanta, Georgia, five years ago. JACOB SCHMIDT (30s), a scientist who works for pharmaceutical company, GeneMede, leaves the office late one night. He hurries to his car with a large wooden box tucked under his arm. He puts it in the trunk, gets in the driver's seat, and locks the door. A bullet barrels through the window and into his head, killing him. The car alarm goes off, scaring the assailant away from the scene.

Blytheville, present day. Though she's been taken off the story, Angie continues her investigation in secret. She researches hybridism as it's laid out in *The Origin of Species*, which leads her to believe that Benjamin Franklin Blythe may have reproduced with his slaves in order to bring his own family's vigor and virility into their bloodline. Stronger slaves mean more work gets done. She reads that one of the abnormalities of this kind of "cross-breeding" is extra digits—six fingers. Could Sallie from her dreams be a descendant of Blythe himself?

Angie's research is interrupted when Blake calls her to tell her a body dating back to the Civil War has been found on the Blytheville state hospital grounds. It sports an execution-style bullet hole in the back of the skull, and the man's bones are big—really big. He was dug up by two men from a shallow grave next to a marker with a number similar to the one Angie fell on.

An autopsy reveals the man has six digits on each hand, and likely had a pituitary gland that was five times the normal size. Evidence shows it had been harvested from his brain by cutting through the mouth's soft palate and chipping through the bone at the back of the throat. These facts are gruesome and puzzling but lead Angie and

Blake to hypothesize these people might have produced a more potent variety of growth hormone, which could be connected to their having extra fingers.

As things start to piece together, Angie and Blake look into GeneMede, which is now big in the DNA game. It was among the first to synthesize human growth hormone in the 1960s, and has a shady history, much of it owing to the unsolved murder of Jacob Schmidt five years prior. The CEO of GeneMede is MAXFIELD BLYTHE OXFORD, a powerful descendant of the Blythe family and cousin to Edgar Blythe, Angie's boss.

As if in direct response to Angie and Blake's revelations, Edgar fires Angie from the paper, and unbeknownst to her, steals her research notebook in the process. Angie finds solace in Blake's arms as he comforts her, and in the process, Blake realizes her home has been bugged. Angie's now caught in the middle of the strange scheme he's investigating. He vows to protect her.

Blake brings the two men who dug up the body at the state hospital in for questioning. They're two dumb thugs who go by FINGERS and BUTTHEAD. After some expert pushing by Blake, they admit they were hired by TED JACKSON to dig up the bones and bug Angie's house.

Jackson is an expert trigger-guy who works for big money and big names. But Blake already knows all about Jackson—he's always been the number one suspect in the GeneMede murder of Jacob Schmidt.

Blake and Angie ask to examine the wooden box that was found at the GeneMede murder scene. It's a cedar box with strange oval symbols carved into it, but the box was never deciphered, and the case never solved. The box is 260 years old, but a piece of vellum that was found inside it is covered with ancient text similar to cuneiform. It's found to be 3,000 years old. It's had the department completely stumped since its discovery, and now seems to be of significance again.

Flashbacks to Africa and then Georgia in 1805 show an African tribe being captured and brought to America as slaves for the Blythe Plantation. The tribe's leader is impregnated by DUNCAN BLYTHE, plantation owner. She gives birth to his child alone in the woods, confused, angry, and helpless. And so begins the line of Blythe/slave hybrids.

Back to present day. MAXFIELD BLYTHE OXFORD, Edgar Blythe, and TED JACKSON all convene in a secret meeting at GeneMede to go through Angie's notebook, stolen by Edgar. Max finds it useless, claiming that putting Angie "on the case" didn't stir up the results he wanted. He dismisses Edgar from his duties and employs Jackson to get his hands on one of the mulattoes, or WATCHERS, that have started to reemerge. Maxfield is trying to get his hands on a piece of their DNA, and Jackson assures Max he can get it—for the greedy price of 10 million dollars. Chump change to Maxfield.

Ted Jackson is a meticulous and bloodthirsty hitman and decides it's time to shake things up. He carefully stalks the GBI Headquarters, looking to take out Blake, his biggest threat. He stakes himself outside headquarters, but when Blake doesn't show up and he begins to fear being recognized, he's forced to settle for agent TOM GORMANN, one of Blake's partners.

He targets Tom by following his son to his soccer game, stealing his jersey, and using pictures of it to persuade Tom via email that if he doesn't give him the information he wants, he has ways of getting to Tom's family. Tom is crushed but has no option but to stay quiet and comply to Jackson's demands—whatever they may be when they come.

After spotting, then losing, Jackson's black Navigator, the GBI now catches wind of Jackson's re-emergence and thinks Angie is his target, so they put her under surveillance protection.

Blake tells Angie he has an overwhelming intuition that something bad is going to happen to him. Blake has always been known for his unusually accurate intuitions, and the severe headaches that come with them. He also tells her they've been sharing the same dreams about Sallie and the other Watchers telling them to persevere. Angie is spooked, more so about Blake's dark premonition than their shared dreams.

As they head to bed that night, Angie looks out the window and spots a black Navigator sitting across the street. She throws her door open to confront the driver, who peels away in a cloud of burning rubber.

EPISODE 3: Fearful that his Navigator is becoming too recognizable, Jackson devises a plan to get rid of it. He ambushes and murders a cab driver and rigs the Navigator to explode with the body inside it, completely annihilating the vehicle while also staging it to look like a terrorist attack. The investigation draws Blake away from Angie for the time being. Blake is pleased to find that Jackson is getting sloppy—a piece of the car that wasn't completely charred helps the GBI identify it as the Navigator. A few droplets of blood and hair left behind during the struggle with the cabbie are recovered. It's the most evidence Jackson has ever left behind.

The GBI holds a press release to shake Jackson up, and it works. Jackson panics when he sees the CNN report with his face plastered all over it. Then he gets a call from Maxfield telling him he's fired. But it only makes him even more determined to eliminate Blake and Angie.

Blake secures a search warrant for the grounds and offices of Blytheville State Hospital, hoping to find something incriminating. He brings Angie with him but instructs her to wait in the car. When the GBI starts their search, Angie spots Flo stepping outside to call someone in a panic—it's Reverend Masterson, but he assures her they won't find anything. And he's right—the GBI turns the place over but finds nothing incriminating, nor anything about the body that was dug up. Another seemingly dead end, and Flo is all-too smug about it.

Determined to get to Jackson any way he can, Blake has FRAN WESTON, director of the DNA division of the GBI, dig back into the Jacob Schmidt GeneMede murder to see if she can come up with anything new on Jackson after five years.

Needing a new lead for her story, Angie interviews REBEKKA HOFFMANN, Reverend Hoffmann's daughter. She's a woman of proud African heritage who misses her dad immensely, still suspicious that his death 34 years earlier was never solved. She's also stepmother to Jacob Schmidt, the scientist who was killed in the GeneMede murder, and suspects the two deaths were somehow connected. But her snooping has been nothing but dead ends after all these years.

Rebekka gives Angie a box full of her father's old research and belongings. The copy of his missing book she owns has been stolen. Rebekka also gives Angie an envelope that Jacob Schmidt instructed her to open upon his death. It contains a single piece of paper with the words "Project Nephili" written on it. Never understanding its significance, it was another dead end for Rebekka and the GBI when they were investigating Jacob's murder.

Blake and Angie explore the contents of the box together, discovering Reverend Hoffman's notes and photographs from his time spent with the Dogon tribes in Africa. The photographs look very much like the Watchers who've been coming to them in their dreams.

November 1864, Blythe Plantation. Duncan Blythe sits with his son Benjamin Franklin Blythe discussing the possibility of Sherman's Army marching on their plantation. As a precaution, Duncan calls upon his most trusted slave GEORGE, a large and dreadlocked mulatto, to help him hide a massive reserve of gold bars in the woods next to the plantation.

Just as they finish, Union soldiers arrive at the plantation and shoot Duncan. With his dying breath, he reveals that George is his grandson and asks him to guard the secret of the gold. But the secret dies with George as the soldiers shoot him, too, and DR. MEDE steps from the group to reveal himself as the mastermind behind their murders, carefully planned out so he can harvest George's pituitary.

Present day. Blake and Angie look over blueprints of the state hospital and Angie notices some of the construction seems to be off—there's likely a hidden wall in the basement of the main building of the hospital. Blake decides to do a solo mission at the hospital that night to see what he can find. Angie begs to come along, but Blake needs to move quickly and silently, so Angie needs to stay behind.

Blake tells only his partner, Tom Gormann, his plans for going back to the hospital, not knowing that Tom is still under Jackson's thumb to give up Blake. Tom begrudgingly tells Jackson that Blake will be alone at the hospital that night. But unable to leave his partner to fend for himself, Tom also heads to the hospital to serve as Blake's backup.

While hiding out near the hospital, Tom's ambushed by CHARLES BUTLER, another of Jackson's recruited henchmen. Charles is the brother of Butthead, one of the thugs who dug up the body on the hospital grounds. Charles knocks Tom out cold before

Jackson arrives. But when Jackson sees that Charles has served his purpose, he turns on him and shoots Charles to rid himself of any witnesses of what he's about to do.

By now, Blake has broken into the hospital and discovered new plaster behind some cabinets in the basement. Behind the plaster is a wall safe. He breaks into the safe and takes out some envelopes and an object wrapped in brown burlap. He quickly stows them in his backpack and leaves to make his getaway, only to come face to face with Jackson. Shots are fired, and Blake buries a slug in Jackson's arm before Jackson plants bullets in Blake's chest and head, leaving him for dead as he rushes off to tend to his own wounds. Blake loses consciousness as his seeping blood pools around him.

EPISODE 4: The GBI investigates the incident at the Hospital. They find Charles's body in the woods, and they find massive blood pools inside—but no bodies. Even though Blake's body is nowhere to be found, his survival is unlikely based on the amount of blood left behind. His backpack is missing, too. Tom is shaken up but keeping his mouth shut about his involvement.

GBI Director ANDREW MCKEE wants to make Tom the lead on this case, but Tom refuses, still feeling too much guilt over Blake's death. Instead, Blake's other partner, Agent JOEY MARTINEZ, is made lead on the case. He delivers the news of Blake's death to Angie. She falls apart. Fran, the DNA director, takes Angie under her wing while she heals emotionally.

Weeks pass with no news of Blake, and Jackson's gone underground. Angie has given up on the hospital story during her stay with Fran, who has proven to be a kind and nurturing woman. After a memorial is finally held for Blake, Angie decides to go back to Blytheville and attempt to pick up the pieces of her life.

In Tel Khirbet Qeiyaga, Israel, it's the spring dig season and AVRAM BENJACOB, a professor of antiquities at Jerusalem University and lead archaeologist on the dig, has uncovered an Iron Age fortified city dating back to the tenth century BCE. The site has only been partially uncovered, but they've found evidence the city was only occupied for roughly twenty years before being strangely abandoned.

They uncover a Massebah at the site, and ELEAZAR BARUCH, a linguistics expert, is called in to decipher the language on it. But it's like nothing he's ever seen before. He guesses it's branched off from an earlier form of cuneiform and developed parallel to but isolated from later script and became a more advanced language. As if in answer to their conundrum, someone from the GBI calls to ask advice about the language on the piece of vellum found in the old cedar box from the Jacob Schmidt GeneMede murder.

Avram determines that the vellum is two millennia older than the writing on the stone they've found, but they don't understand how that's possible if it became a dead language after the city was abandoned. But they're able to use the vellum to start translating the Massebah, putting the importance of it on par with the discovery of the Rosetta Stone.

During their translation, they repeatedly find the word "king." From context, it seems to be in reference to King Anakim, the king of the Nephilim, biblical beings said to be the "sons of God" and the "daughters of men."

In Blytheville, Angie takes a waitressing job to slowly get her life back on track after the heartbreak of losing Blake. Jackson catches wind of her returning home and sets out to eliminate her to tie up loose ends. He breaks into her home one night, but she's not there. In his frustration, he empties six bullets into her mirror before leaving. His paranoia and anxiety are causing him to unravel.

Joey and Tom investigate the break-in. They discover the bullets Jackson left behind are a match to the bullet that killed Jacob Schmidt five years ago. They're getting closer to Jackson, they can feel it.

Angie dives back into her research of the hospital with renewed vigor. She reexamines the box of items from Rebekka, and notices something glistening over the "i" on the paper reading "Project Nephili." Fran runs tests and discovers it's a tiny piece of microfilm with an unknown DNA gene sequence written into it.

That night, Angie arrives home late from work to find Blake's missing backpack on her porch. Then, after four long months, Blake appears. He's in an almost hypnotic daze, unable to remember where he's been, why he's back, or how he's alive.

EPISODE 5: Ted Jackson continues to lose his cool. He hides out in a storage facility, gets a new weapon from a pawnshop, changes his appearance, and continues to stalk Tom Gormann and his family. His daily manic panic attacks deteriorate his health. He's quickly unravelling under the threat of being caught for all the crimes he's committed over the years.

Angie and Blake investigate what might have happened to Blake by going through his backpack. It contains the contents from the safe at the hospital, including Rebekka's stolen copy of her father's book *Come to Me You Who Labor and Are Heavy Laden.* It's the object Angie watched Reverend Masterson take from his bank and to the hospital in a panic the day she interviewed and then followed him.

They dig through the old photographs in the box and discover one of Sallie, the woman they see in their dreams. There are photographs dating back to when the hospital was a plantation and a lime quarry. Reverend Hofmann collected extensive evidence and research to back up the horrid stories and claims he wrote in his book.

They also find old census reports from the plantation and discover that the Blythe men were breeding with their slaves. The trend shows that the slaves gradually got bigger in size and most were mulatto and fathered by Blythe.

Hospital therapy records show Dr. Mede was performing experimental shock and drug therapy on pre-pubescent children who were mulatto and polydactyl—obvious descendants of Sallie's family. Though the tests were dangerous, Dr. Mede was seemingly onto something. His treatments resulted in significant growth spurts in the children over a short period of time—as long as they survived.

But after 1946, the experiments tapered off and there were no mulattoes involved. Blake and Angie guess that Sallie's descendants must have gone into hiding after Mede discovered their growth hormones have a genetic switch that was turned on by shock therapy. It's something that would be extremely valuable to a pharmaceutical company. GeneMede must be deeply involved with the hospital's history because they were—and still are—desperate to obtain these genetic capabilities.

Blythe County, Georgia, 1910. HOMER (the body dug up on the Hospital grounds) lives a peaceful life as a free slave, going out of his way to be friendly and helpful to his community. But his compassion gets him nowhere when he's wrongfully accused of lewdness toward women and sentenced to labor camp as punishment. It's then that Dr. Mede reveals himself to once again be the one behind the entire scheme, and he kills Homer, so he can harvest his pituitary and run a series of procedures to turn it into a liquid that he injects into himself. Little does Mede know that Homer is the last of Sallie's known descendants.

EPISODE 6: Present day, Blytheville. Tom Gormann is requested at the Blythe County Penitentiary—Butthead, one of the street thugs

206

hired by Jackson, wants to talk to him. Butthead has found out that his brother, Charles Butler, has been killed by Jackson, and he's pissed. He's ready to not only rat out Jackson, but also play a hand in bringing him down in any way he can.

In Blake's latest dream about Sallie and her people, they tell him they were the ones who saved him after he was shot by Jackson. This propels him and Angie to crack open Reverend Hofmann's book, which chronicles his time spent at the asylum and recounts lynching, disappearances, conscription into prison labor, horrifyingly harmful medical experiments, white-on-black rape, and no one being brought to justice for any of it. They're determined to get it republished. They know—can feel—that the Watchers must be real, alive, and thriving somewhere deep in hiding, and that he and Angie need to find them before GeneMede or Jackson does. And they realize they can't do it alone.

They call in Tom and Joey, who are amazed and relieved to see Blake is alive. Tom's emotions come crashing down and he finally admits to Blake that Jackson almost killing him was his fault, that he's been under the man's thumb. Blake is forgiving but has no choice but to suspend Tom temporarily for breaking protocol.

Blake then meets with McKee, the GBI director, and gives him the low-down on everything that's happened, revealing all his suspicions, conclusions, and strange hunches, even talking about his dreams of Sallie and the Watchers. But McKee doesn't think Blake's crazy—just the opposite. Sallie has also made an appearance in one of his dreams—apparently, she's covering all her bases. They agree to put their combined forces behind bringing down Jackson and GeneMede once and for all.

The team narrows down the location of Jackson's storage facility by analyzing the photo of Tom Gormann's son's soccer jersey, based on a reflection of a garage door and a car in the photo. At the same time, the sequencing from Jacob Schmidt's Project Nephili microfilm comes back: it's a gene for a protein almost identical to human growth hormone. Jacob Schmidt had worked out the sequence of the Watchers' special hormone under the GeneMede radar during his time with them, but knowing the value and danger of it falling into the wrong hands, he snuck the secret gene through the note to his mother. But the remaining question is: Is this the human growth hormone that's been at the center of this case? If so, how did Jacob get his hands on it? Is it possible that he was in touch with the Watchers a mere five years ago?

EPISODE 7: Joey and Tom have arranged for Butthead to help them flush Jackson out. They wire Butthead and have him set up a meeting with Jackson, who's now so hell-bent on finally taking Blake out that he agrees to meet because Butthead claims to know where Blake is. Jackson's quickly-unraveling nerves continue to push him closer and closer to psychosis.

With the GBI hiding in place, Butthead and Jackson meet, and Butthead nudges him into revealing that he killed Jacob Schmidt and that Maxfield Oxford hired him to do it. But Butthead's anger gets the better of him and he attacks Jackson, effectively ending the "interview." Jackson is taken into custody and finally suffers a full-blown catatonic meltdown, becoming completely unresponsive to stimuli. Blake's sense of aura creeps back into his mind and he can't help but feel that he's somehow caused Jackson's strange response to finally being caught.

Meanwhile at the dig site in Israel, an astrological team working alongside the archaeological team discover there's an elliptical wall surrounding the 3200 BCE city they're digging and provide coordinates to the mathematical epicenter of the ellipse. Historically, important location or artifacts are buried at these kinds of epicenters, and they're determined to uncover what might be there.

But the team faces trouble getting clearance to dig at the coordinated epicenter of their ancient city wall because uncovering the city of the Nephilim in Israel might alter what is widely historically and religiously accepted by most professionals; their five-thousand-year-old pagan city doesn't fit into the world view of those who need to approve their digging.

So Avram and Eleazar use a ground-penetrating radar to glimpse what might be under the ground at the location. They're shocked to find a tomb, because in Israel, burials then were in ossuaries, not tombs; they're not in Egypt. Nothing about this dig fits with the history of the land they currently know. They're convinced they've discovered an unknown early monotheistic culture that may add an entirely new chapter to the Judeo-Christian tradition. Their board of directors can't say no to letting them dig the site now.

As they dig, it becomes completely apparent that the magnificent city site was abandoned and the tomb was covered, but they don't understand why. When they finally reach the tomb, they realize they've found Nefertiti's burial site, a highly coveted but never discovered tomb. They had expected to find the King of the Nephilim inside this tomb, and instead they find a queen. But her tomb isn't lavish and exquisite like King Tut or other rulers of the time.

ASAR BAKHOUM, head of Egypt's Supreme Council of Antiquities, is brought in as a guest to the dig to witness the opening of the tomb and he's less-than-thrilled that finding Nefertiti's tomb in Israel suggests she may have been part Jewish rather than full Egyptian. They hypothesize that she likely ruled in Egypt, but her body was returned to Israel upon her death.

Her tomb also reveals a mix of hieroglyphs and the cuneiform-like language they've been deciphering. Not to mention that Nefertiti seems to have been much taller than anticipated, and that she was at least 110 years old when she died. She also has six fingers on each hand.

EPISODE 8: Blake and Angie are visited by LEON, a geneticist and one of Sallie's people—a live Watcher in the flesh. He's been watching over them and helping where he could at every major event they've experienced over the last few months. He tells them that his people have a special intuition and way of communicating, and that's why they've been able to come to them in their dreams.

Leon worked with Jacob Schmidt to sequence his own DNA. When things started to go sour with GeneMede, they were forced to hide their discovery. Their plan now is to patent the sequence and assign it to a trust with Rebekka Hoffmann as the trustee. Before he leaves, Leon also reveals that he and his people are indeed the Nephilim.

The GBI now has Jackson, but because he's unable to talk due to his strange state, they need to come up with a new plan to nail Maxfield Oxford. They decide to squeeze Max's assistant GORDON SMITHSON by telling him Jackson will provide new evidence in the Jacob Schmidt murder that will implicate him as an accomplice.

Gordon fears for his life in helping them, but they offer protection in exchange for all the documents they want, plus access to Jackson's encrypted computer files. Gordon caves and confirms Max's connection to Jackson, that he hired him to find the Watchers and take out anyone who gets in his way.

The GBI finally has access to all of GeneMede's records and emails that implicate its years of crime, able to secure search warrants and freeze accounts. They dig up more bodies on the hospital grounds, all slaves and descendants of Watchers. With their case built, the GBI raids Maxfield's office—but he's one step ahead of them again and shoots himself before they can get to him.

With her journalistic gears grinding again, Angie has completed her story on the entirety of the convoluted history of Blytheville State Hospital and sold it to the *Associated Press* for $50,000.

Angie gets a call from Reverend Masterson, wants to meet with her in the nursing home at Blytheville State. Flo Dobson, who's had a stroke, and Ted Jackson, still in his catatonic state, are now residents at the Hospital along with Masterson. Masterson apologizes to Angie and admits to the role he played in the gruesomeness of the hospital all those years. Flo feels deep remorse for her role, too.

Masterson also reveals that he's 121 years old, Flo is 116, and Dr. Mede, miraculously still alive at 162 years old, is also secretly living in the nursing home under an alias. Along with Maxfield Oxford, who was 111 when he died, they've been using stores of the harvested pituitaries to create longevity for themselves. If only Angie hadn't already turned in her story…

Leon returns to bring Blake and Angie to meet the rest of the Nephilim—they've been living in an advanced community in a large limestone cave beneath the closed and dilapidated negro ward of the Hospital. They finally meet Sallie, who tells them that in 1907 her people found hundreds of gold bars hidden in this cave and that's how they were able to build their secret city.

Sallie gives them a tour, showing them their super-advanced technological and medical practices, including the facility where they saved Blake's life after they rescued him from Jackson's attack. Sallie then invites them to participate in a holy holiday that night, celebrating the conjunction of the star Sirius with the Sun, as represented by the elliptical symbol originally tacked to Angie's door.

In the Epilogue, Flo wraps a plastic bag around Dr. Mede's head as he sits helplessly in his wheelchair. Masterson chuckles as he watches Mede finally pay for his gruesome life.

CHARACTERS:

ANGIE MCDOWELL: Investigative journalist working at *The Blytheville Express* after being fired from a bigger publication due to excessive alcohol abuse.

BLAKE CHILDS: A pathologist and field agent for the Georgia Bureau of Investigation. Angie's love interest.

TED JACKSON: A ruthless hired hitman with a history of murder in Blytheville with a personal vendetta against Blake Childs, who's never been able to gather enough evidence to bring him to justice. Jackson lingers on the border of insanity fueled by paranoia and poor health.

MAXFLIED BLYTHE OXFORD: President and CEO of GeneMede, a hugely wealthy Atlanta-based pharmaceutical company under scrutiny for questionable research. Ted Jackson is his hired hitman.

SALLIE: Leader of the "Watchers," descendants of the Nephilim who were Blythe slaves for hundreds of years until their apparent disappearance several decades ago.

FLO DOBSON: A former nurse at the Blytheville State Hospital, she's now retired and working as a housekeeper and tour guide for the hospital.

REVEREND SHELDON MASTERSON: The unofficial town historian who used to work at the hospital.

DR. MEDE: Head doctor at the Blytheville State Hospital who ruthlessly killed Watchers in order to harvest their pituitary for study and personal medical use.

TOM GORMANN: One of Blake Childs' partners at the GBI. A family man with a wife and young son.

JOEY MARTINEZ: One of Blake Childs' partners at the GBI.

FRAN WESTON: Head of the DNA department of the GBI.

ANDREW MCKEE: Director of the GBI.

AVRAM BENJACOB: A professor of antiquities at Jerusalem University and lead archaeologist on the Israel dig.

ELEAZAR BARUCH: A linguistics expert called in to decipher the language found at the Israel dig.

BENJAMIN FRANKLIN BLYTHE: Former owner of the Blythe Plantation, who owned the Watchers as slaves.

DUNCAN BLYTHE: Former owner of the Blythe Plantation and BFJ's father. He had sex with his slaves in order to produce virility in them and to continue the line of Watchers.

RUTHERFORD HOFFMANN: Chaplain at the Hospital for 25 years. He wrote a book documenting the horrors of treatment and experiments of patients at the hospital. No copies of his book can be found anymore. He died under mysterious circumstances. He is Rebekka Hoffmann's father.

REBEKKA HOFFMANN: Rutherford Hoffmann's daughter and Jacob Schmidt's stepmother. She is in possession of all her father's research about the Plantation and Hospital, as well as the last known copy of his book.

JACOB SCHMIDT: A former GeneMede geneticist found murdered in the GeneMede parking lot five years prior. He's also Rebekka Hoffman's stepson.

FINGERS: A street thug hired by Ted Jackson to dig up Homer's body on the hospital grounds.

BUTTHEAD: A street thug hired by Ted Jackson to dig up Homer's body on the hospital grounds. His brother is Charles Butler.

CHARLES BUTLER: A street thug hired by Ted Jackson to assist him in his attempted murder of Blake Childs. Jackson turns on him and murders him, sending his brother Butthead into a rage.

HOMER: A slave on the Blytheville Plantation in its heyday, who eventually became a free man that was wrongfully prosecuted for lewd behavior, and plot devised by Dr. Mede in order to kill him for his pituitary gland.

LEON: One of the Watchers that acts as a liaison between their group and Angie and Blake.

EDGAR BLYTHE: Editor-in-Chief at *The Blytheville Express*. Has deep roots in the Blythe family and is Maxfield Blythe Oxford's cousin.

GORDON SMITHSON: Maxfield Blythe Oxford's assistant.

BUDDY ZANE: One of Ted Jackson's hired henchmen assigned to kill Angie. When he fails, Jackson kills him.

APPENDIX D:

Sample Budget Top Sheet

PRELIM DISCUSSION BUDGET 002

US Dollar Budget (CND @0.82)
Prep Weeks - 4
Shoot Days 20

Shoot Location: Vancouver Island, BC, Canada
Post Location: Vancouver, BC, Canada
Unions: SAG/UBCP/DGC

Acc#	Category Description	Page	Total
0100	STORY RIGHTS/ACQUISITIONS	1	$86,150
0200	SCENARIO	1	$90,977
0300	DEVELOPMENT COSTS	1	$80,000
0400	PRODUCER	1	$290,976
0500	DIRECTOR	2	$131,072
0600	STARS	2	$647,048
	TOTAL "A"		**$1,327,322**
1000	CAST	5	$252,283
1100	EXTRAS	6	$109,419
1200	PRODUCTION STAFF	7	$248,493
1300	DESIGN LABOUR	10	$40,163
1400	CONSTRUCTION LABOUR	10	$18,149
1500	SET DRESSING LABOUR	11	$40,931
1600	PROPERTY LABOUR	11	$36,682
1800	WRANGLER LABOUR	12	$2,577
1900	WARDROBE LABOUR	12	$51,351
2000	MAKEUP/HAIR LABOUR	13	$29,314
2200	CAMERA LABOUR	14	$93,939
2300	ELECTRICAL LABOUR	15	$39,733
2400	GRIP LABOUR	16	$35,213
2500	PRODUCTION SOUND LABOUR	17	$22,194
2600	TRANSPORTATION LABOUR	18	$88,186
2800	PROD.OFFICE EXPENSES	20	$45,920
3100	SITE EXPENSES	20	$152,466
3200	UNIT EXPENSES	23	$52,392
3300	TRAVEL & LIVING EXPENSES	23	$182,396
3400	TRANSPORTATION	25	$102,452
3500	CONSTRUCTION MATERIALS	29	$8,150
3600	ART SUPPLIES	29	$2,050
3700	SET DRESSING	29	$30,200
3800	PROPS	30	$11,767
4000	ANIMALS	30	$2,460
4100	WARDROBE SUPPLIES	30	$22,181
4200	MAKEUP/HAIR SUPPLIES	31	$2,060
4500	CAMERA EQUIPMENT	31	$26,438
4600	ELECTRICAL EQUIPMENT	31	$29,520
4700	GRIP EQUIPMENT	32	$31,078
4800	SOUND EQUIPMENT	32	$14,809
4900	SECOND UNIT	33	$4,209
5100	PRODUCTION LABORATORY	33	$2,050
	TOTAL PRODUCTION "B"		**$1,831,217**
6000	EDITORIAL LABOUR	34	$155,323
6100	EDITORIAL EQUIPMENT	34	$45,674
6600	MUSIC	35	$51,047
6800	VERSIONING	35	$11,525
	TOTAL POST PRODUCTION "C"		**$263,570**
7000	UNIT PUBLICITY	37	$12,628
7100	GENERAL EXPENSES	37	$43,546
7200	INDIRECT COSTS	37	$205,000
7300	CANADIAN TAX CREDITS	38	$(553,500)
	TOTAL OTHER "D"		**$(292,324)**
8100	COMPLETION GURANTEE		$75,000
8200	CONTINGENCY		$150,000
	Total Above-The-Line		**$1,327,322**
	Total Below-The-Line		**$1,802,463**
	Total Above and Below-The-Line		**$3,129,784**
	GRAND TOTAL –		**$3,354,784**

ABOUT THE AUTHORS

DR. KENNETH ATCHITY'S lifelong core expertise is stories. He's edited them, taught them, developed them, sold them (yes, for millions!), produced them—and written them. Most of all, he delights in storytelling as he moves from restaurant to bar to publishing  office in Manhattan, or from studio to agencies to management companies to screenings in Los Angeles—all the while listening to stories, retelling stories, and selling stories. His life as a story merchant isn't all that different from his years growing up, driving from one town in Louisiana to another, visiting aunts who would compete to feed him and uncles who competed to tell him the most memorable stories.

He became good at the vocation of story merchandising because (a) he understands what makes a marketable story and (b) his passion for the art of storytelling is unbounded because (c) he believes in the power of stories to change the world. "Hollywood," he likes to say,  "is the one place where you can die of enthusiasm. But they haven't been able to kill me yet because enthusiasm is rebirth for me—and it happens every time I find a great new story!"

On the set of *Angels in the Snow*, Vancouver

Author of two dozen books, longtime reviewer for the *Los Angeles Times* Book Review, professor of literature, literary manager, career coach, and motion picture and television producer, Ken has spoken, workshopped, lectured, and keynoted about storytelling and the story market at dozens of universities, writers' conferences, at high schools, grade schools, and adult education centers throughout the US, Asia, and Europe.

What does Ken know that others don't? He knows how to pitch a story with enthusiasm and get the "checkbooks" to read and respond to it. It's taken him forty years to know where the checkbooks are, which is why the advice offered in this book is invaluable. It's not just storytelling theory; it's storytelling practice as observed by someone who sells and produces stories for a living.

His favorite refrain, even when it's accompanied by a "no," is, "You always send us great stories. Can't wait for the next one." His advice to would-be professional storytellers is:

1. Get through the no's as quickly as you can because you only need one yes.
2. Never give up!
3. Publish it direct!

 IN 1999, LISA CERASOLI wrote her first feature film—a romantic comedy—while under contract on a series as an actor. Shortly thereafter, Lionsgate took interest. The movie never made it to production, but it did lead to a meeting with Ken, as she was looking for representation as a writer. He read her script and dared her to turn it into a book. Two weeks and three chapters later, she was hooked on creative writing. Since then, Ken has been her literary manager and mentor. Over the course of working closely with him as the editor of her novel and memoir, their relationship evolved. They are now long-time colleagues and friends, and as of this book, partners in writing.

Lisa has been working as Ken's VP at Story Merchant since 2013.

For the authors who have books they can envision on the big and small screens, Lisa serves as a bridge, assisting, advising, as well as writing, developing, and editing every step of the way. Shortly after joining Ken's team, Lisa started 529 Books, a Story Merchant sister company, for authors writing nonfiction and those interested in self-publishing.

Lisa and Ken: Thrillerfest after-party, New York City

Thanks in great part to Ken's guidance, Lisa has been fortunate to collaborate with hundreds of talented authors, making their publishing dreams a reality. Working full-time in the industry has allowed her to stay up-to-date with its ever-expanding tendencies. "Ask me anything!" No, really, she loves assisting authors, never tires of industry questions, and promises nothing excites her more than a great story.

Lisa has authored and co-authored numerous books (eight and counting) and directed a documentary short, which she executive produced with Ken. Collectively, her

works have garnered over twenty-five national and international awards, and her memoir has been optioned for a series. Lisa lives with her thirteen-year-old daughter, Jazz, and two adorable Yorkie Poos (that Jazz talked her into) in Marquette, Michigan, a charming town built on the shores of Lake Superior. When she's not discussing *all things* storytelling, or telling one herself, Lisa enjoys watching Jazz play basketball and introducing her to John Hughes' films and classic TV, such as *I Love Lucy, The Golden Girls,* and *The Wonder Years.*

Practicing yoga, trail running, and playing floor hockey and Euchre with her gal pals are other favorite pastimes.

CHELSEA MONGIRD is the current Vice President of Operations for Dr. Atchity's three companies: Story Merchant Books, Atchity Productions, and The Writer's Lifeline. She's read, edited, and developed hundreds of scripts and manuscripts, and continues to work as a development executive and producer on the dozens of film and television projects currently on the companies' slates. Along with managing the production details of publishing Story Merchant Books, she also educates and instructs the companies' intern and editing teams on achieving strong story-building skills and critical reading analysis. It's a challenge to find a genre that doesn't fascinate or inspire Chelsea, but her deepest passion is for children's stories and animated films—something she attributes to wanting to bring a little fun to a world that sometimes takes itself too seriously.

Filming in Downtown San Diego

To Our Readers:

Thank you for taking the time to read this book. We sincerely hope it helps you, and we want to make each edition more helpful than the last. Please review it for us on www.amazon.com.

If the mood strikes, please send us an email with comments or suggestions for improving this guide in any way. Feel free to mention your writing endeavors and achievements or tell us about your "day job" and your career ambitions as a storyteller. Who knows, we may be able to make a connection for you!

Email info:

atchity@storymerchant.com

or

lisacerasoli@gmail.com

For an overview of Atchity's film career, visit:
http://www.imdb.com/name/nm0040338/?ref_=fn_al_nm_1

For Cerasoli's:
http://www.imdb.com/name/nm0148453/?ref_=fn_al_nm_1

For professional editing or ghostwriting services:
www.thewriterslifeline.com

For representation or personal one-on-one coaching from
Dr. Atchity:
www.storymerchant.com

To direct-publish your book with us:
www.storymerchantbooks.com

STORY MARKET TERMS

A-list: Metaphorical reference to the top writers, directors, or stars in Hollywood.

Above-the-line: The first part of an entertainment budget that covers the cost of dramatic rights, producers', director, and principal talent.

Act break: The scene before the present act ends and the next act begins, usually strikingly dramatic as with a cliffhanger or unexpected twist.

Acquisition editors: The executives at a traditional publishing house who read incoming manuscripts and announce the decision of whether they will be accepted or rejected.

Acquisition meeting: Usually held on Monday morning, the meeting where the story editors pitch the executives on stories they've rated as "recommend" and answer queries, if any, about stories they are *not* recommending.

Action: The physical act of doing something to achieve an aim.

Acts: Drama, of which film is a most prodigious subset, has a beginning, middle, and end that are loosely known as "acts." Although the three-act structure has been around since the classical Greeks, the number of acts can also be four (preferred, for example, by Todd Klick's *Beat by Beat*), five (as in Renaissance dramas, including Shakespeare and Marlowe), or even seven (used by network television movies). What's happening in these variances is that act two, which I refer to in one of my books as the "Serengeti Plain" because it punishes so many dramatists with its seemingly interminable length compared to act one and the final act, is simply being divided to make it easier to conquer. In other words, in a network film, act two is divided into act two, act three, act four, act five, and act six, leaving act seven to bring us a satisfying conclusion.

Adaptation: A movie, television drama, or stage play that has been adapted from a previous written work, typically from a novel or nonfiction book or magazine article.

Advance: Money paid upon execution of a contract for transfer of intellectual property from the creator to the publisher. In the film industry, this is referred to as an *option payment*.

Agent, agency: A writer's representative who sells his or her client's stories to studios, producers, or broadcasters for a commission of ten percent.

Allegory: A story that reveals a message or moral beneath its surface.

Ally: The protagonist's companion, who assists him in achieving his mission or quest. Wizards, tricksters, old soldiers, retired martial arts masters are examples of allies.

Ancillary rights: the rights beyond the primary ones that bring extra income to the storyteller. For example, greeting card or comic books rights ancillary to the primary novel publishing rights, or to the primary screenplay production rights.

Animation: A medium in which images are shaped and reshaped to appear as though moving.

Anime: Originating in Japan, a style of computer or hand-drawn animation reminiscent of comic books.

Antagonist: The character who acts against the protagonist and tries to defeat him; an adversary.

Anticlimax: A scene that follows the climax of a novel or film, reducing the climax's impact.

Antihero: Like the reluctant hero, a protagonist without the heroic elements normally associated with a hero.

Arc: The trajectory of a character's development in drama from A to Z, from its opening position to the position he or she occupies at the story's end. See **character arc.**

Archetype: The original story element that perfectly fits the character, place, or theme. For example, Odysseus is the archetypal wandering hero, while *The Odyssey* is the archetype of the homecoming story.

Arena: The subject matter or setting of a story—the South Pole, the dark side of the moon, the Planet Mars, or a law office.

Attach, attachment: As in "attach a lead actor," is a term that means a deal has been made and signed with an element needed for a motion picture, detailing the actor's compensation and the start date of the film. A typical question might be, "Is Jennifer Lawrence just interested, or is she attached?"

Auction: A sales event in which a number of buyers are orchestrated to bid against one another to maximize the amount paid for intellectual rights.

Back end: When all the expenses associated with a film have been paid off and the investors recouped, we've reached the back end. Which is where "profits" come in.

Backdoor pilot: A television movie that becomes so popular its producers are able to find a broadcaster to relaunch the story as an ongoing series.

Background: The area or scenery behind the main object of attention, especially when perceived as a framework for it.

Backstory: The story behind the story, or before the story, that explains the characters' actions in the story itself.

Baggage: Personnel elements attached to an intellectual property as a condition of its sale and/or production.

Bankable: A film, star, or director whose box office success is so great a studio or financer will immediately agree to financing.

Bankable films include the James Bond franchise, stars include Tom Hanks, and directors include Steven Spielberg.

Beat: A basic action point in a story; in a screenwriting, a pause indicated before or after a piece of dialogue.

Beat sheet: A writing tool used to identify the sequence of events, and actions in your story. It is an abbreviated way to break down the structure of your story, making it easier to organize and change. The beat sheet charts the sequence of events that cause your main character to do something and maps how your main character changes from the beginning to the end of your story. Create a beat sheet by using bullet points that illustrate in one or two lines the order of your plot's progression. Remember plot takes place when a character does something or acts upon another character.

Beginning: The opening or start of a story, ideally a hook that draws the reader or audience into it.

Below-the-line: Entertainment budgets are divided into Above-the-line which includes rights, talent, directing, and producing and Below-the-line that includes all the professional personnel required to make the film.

Bestseller: A book that has sold sufficient units to appear on a nationally-recognized "bestseller list."

Bible: A full, often-illustrated, proposal for a television series or limited series that lays out in detail the overview of the story, the principal characters, the supporting characters, the setting, and a treatment of the pilot and first several episodes, along with an overview of seasons subsequent to the first season.

Bidding war: What happens when several buyers keep increasing their bids to secure rights to an intellectual property until only one is left (the purchaser).

Blockbuster: A very successful movie.

Book blogger: Bloggers who review and comment on books.

Box office: Revenues taken in through tickets sold to moviegoers who physically attend a theater to see a film.

Bridge: Something intended to reconcile or form a connection between two elements in a story.

Bridge financing: Financing that expects to be recouped against other incoming financing. See **Gap financing.**

Broad comedy: Comedy that uses physical, crass, and stupid humor to appeal to the broadest possible audience.

Cameo: A small role in a motion picture, often given to a meaningful name in order to heighten the film's profile.

Catharsis (catharsis): Referred to by drama critics from Aristotle to Wordsworth as the "purgation of emotions" that occurs when a drama is effectively-constructed, as when the audience of a horror film scream and release their fear at the climax of the movie.

Chapter: A cohesive section of a book, usually either titled or numbered or both, dealing with a single facet of the subject at hand (nonfiction) or a sequence of progressive scenes (in fiction).

Character: The artistic facsimile of a human being constructed by the author in a novel, play, or movie as part of a dramatic story, with behavioral elements or traits that make him or her dramatically interesting.

Character arc: How a character changes from beginning to end is called the "arc." With a minor character, it can take as few as three scenes to define them. A major character makes slower progress along his or her arc.

Cinema, cinematic: Generic term for motion pictures, and also the theaters where they're exhibited.

Cliffhanger: The moment at the end of an act when the storyteller places the character, actually or metaphorically, at the edge of a cliff—luring the audience to "stay tuned" to see what happens next.

Climax: Act three of a screenplay weaves all threads of its dramatic action together in a climax that brings the story to a satisfying resolution.

Collaboration: The act of writing a story together, ideally based on an agreement that lays out the exact details of who does what and who gets what, as in "collaboration agreement."

Comedy: A story, normally with a happy ending, that makes the audience laugh. In ancient Greek theater, a comedy always ended in a wedding.

Comic: Causing or meant to cause laughter.

Coming of age: A story that dramatizes the pivotal moment when a child becomes an adult.

Compensated: Compensation, i.e., being *paid,* comes in two forms: front-end, a payment that occurs upon either signing a contract or upon the start of filming, or both; and back-end, which includes both "contingent compensation," covering what happens if your film leads to a sequel or prequel, a television series, or a remake—and profit participation, which gives you a share in the producer's revenues from the film.

Completion bond: A financial agreement from a guarantor that he will assume the responsibility for completing the film on budget and on time. Though the bonding company works hand in hand with the producers and director, it holds the absolute power to take over the filming if necessary, to accomplish that goal. The takeover rarely has to happen.

Complication: A storytelling term to describe what happens when one dramatic obstacle in the protagonist's journey turns out to open into more than one complication, leaving the protagonist further conflicted.

Concept: The idea that generates a story, sometimes called the "what if," as in "What if a king decided to test his three daughters' love for him by offering to divide his kingdom according to which of them loves him most?"

Conclusion: Following the climax, the end point of a story that resolves all its elements one way or another.

Conflict: A serious disagreement or argument, when two forces are pitted against each other.

Connections: A relationship in which a person, thing, or idea is linked or associated with something else.

Contingent compensation: Your negotiated share of the profits of a film.

Coproduction deal: When two producers decide to produce a film together, the agreement they enter into is called a coproduction deal, outlining what each is contributing to the project, the responsibilities of each, and the participation and credits contemplated for each.

Courtesy Read: Entertainment industry term for offering to read a submitted story simply as a courtesy based on who the writer is with no particular regard for acquiring it for production.

Coverage: A professional reader's report on a story that gives the exec who commissioned the coverage an overall view of it as a commercial project, starting with its logline, synopsis, character analysis, dialogue analysis, plot analysis, and including a recommendation: PASS/RECOMMEND/CONSIDER/CONSIDER WITH DEVELOPMENT.

Creative dialogue: The interaction between producers, actors, director and the screenwriter in which notes are proposed, discussed, and either implemented or put aside.

Credit: If you're a writer, your "credit" on a film is determined only by the Writers Guild of America's accreditation committee. In Hollywood, credits are as important as money so make sure you've got a good attorney who will fight for the credit you deserve.

Crisis: The final turning point in a story, when the protagonist must take an action or make a decision that will resolve the mission.

Crossover: A term used variously to mean a story that uses elements of more than one genre, as in a sci-fi comedy; or a project that meets the needs of more than one market, as when *The Bridges of Madison Country* satisfied both the romance and mainstream markets.

Dailies: In today's digital world, the term describes the unedited footage shot in making a motion picture. Sometimes called rushes.

Deal memo: Any document that records an agreement in the entertainment industries.

Deferred payment: A payment that is made "later," for example, instead of "upon principal photography," it's paid from back-end revenues.

Demographics: Data that defines the particular audience for a publishing or entertainment project, as in "white female over 40," or "Hispanics under 21."

Denouement: The last section of a story that brings all the elements to resolution.

Deus ex machina: Latin term ("god from a chariot") that disparagingly refers to a story element that solves a dramatic conflict by introducing an element that isn't in the cast of characters introduced to date.

Development: The process by which an intellectual property (idea, treatment, book, ineffective screenplay, etc.) is transformed into an acceptable shooting script.

Development Hell: When a film languishes at a studio or production company and has yet to reach the day of principal photography (the first day of shooting), and that's gone on for a year or more, you're officially in development hell. One of our films had four sets of writers involved, four directors, two stars, and still hasn't made it to the screen…yet.

Dialogue: Conversation between two or more characters to move the action of a story forward.

Dialogue tags: A small phrase either before, after, or in between the actual dialogue itself.

Diction: The "choice of words," the selection of vocabulary by which a character or mood is defined or tone of voice established.

Direct-published, direct publishing: Authors, assisted or otherwise, who publish their books directly to the distribution outlet, like the internet, without going through the traditional publishing system.

Distributor: A company that delivers motion pictures to their audiences, whether by screen, streaming, or sale to a broadcast company and charges a "distribution fee" for doing so.

Domestic distributor: A film distributor who places your finished film in theaters, or releases it television, or in both markets, in the United States and Canada.

Drabble: A short work of fiction of around one hundred words in length.

Drama: A play for theater, radio, television, or new media that shows characters involved in an exciting conflicted action.

Dramatic rights: The rights to dramatize a story or other intellectual property.

Dramatis personae: The list of "players" or characters traditionally shown at the beginning of a play for legitimate theater.

Ensemble piece: A drama without a protagonist, but which has several characters playing equally important roles.

Epilogue: A section or speech at the end of a book or play that serves as a comment on or conclusion to what happened in the story.

Episodic: A storytelling unit that forms part of a larger story. Episodic TV includes series like *Scandal* or *Revenge*, and miniseries like *American Dynasty: The Kennedys*.

Equity or equity investment: A term that in most businesses means a risk investment of actual capital into a project that has no guaranteed certainty of breaking even. In the film business, equity is structured as a loan to the film, repayable plus a fixed rate, from revenues. But it is still actually at-risk actual or leveraged capital committed solely to the film's production.

E-novelist: A novelist whose platform is digital, i.e., an e-book.

Establish: To introduce, as in "Establish the Alaskan wilderness" or "Establish the protagonist in the midst of a rainstorm."

Executive Producer: In film, a producer that provides a significant portion of financing, or that provides and/or develops the underlying property, for a motion picture production; in television, the producer who oversees the production of a movie or series, often the writer. "Executive producer" is a higher title in television than "producer," and a lower title than "producer" in film.

Expertise: Skill or knowledge in a given field based on experience.

Exhibitor: A theater or chain of theaters that shows or exhibits motion pictures to ticket-buying audiences.

Exposition: The laying out of the obligatory elements of a story that ideally occurs, dramatically, in the first third of the story.

Feature film: Generally, a full-length motion picture that's exhibited in theaters.

Festival circuit: An extensive network of independent film festivals across a specific community, nation, or world.

Film noir: A style of film featuring dreary, fatalistic, or gloomy settings and/or characters. Frequently feature detectives, espionage, and rain like *Sunset Boulevard* or *L.A. Confidential*.

Film stock: The physical blank film upon which the camera creates images during filmmaking. Since films often don't use a portion of a reel of film, extra film is sometimes available for postproduction facilities to sell or donate.

First-person narrative: Term for a story in which the narrator, who's telling the story, into the story so he's a character in it.

Fish out of water: A type of story that puts the protagonist into a world or arena alien to him, as in *The Shape of Water* or *The Martian* or *The Little Mermaid*.

Fixed compensation: The contractual amount paid for the dramatic rights to an underlying intellectual property (I.P.), as opposed to "contingent compensation." The I.P. contracted for includes the script and every preceding form of the story it is based on or inspired by.

Fluff: Writing considered trivial or superficial.

Foreshadowing: A story element that hints at or foreshadows a future story element.

Fourth wall: A storytelling term that describes the separation between the reader or audience from the events of the story; it's a wall that the audience sees through but the actors, supposedly, do not though "piercing the fourth wall" occurs to great effect in *House of Cards* when Kevin Spacey looks at and talks to the camera, or when Don Quixote and Sancho Panza read about their adventures in Miguel de Cervantes' *Don Quixote: Part Two*.

Franchise: An established brand featuring the same character and/or theme, like the Bond movies, *Spiderman,* or *The Pink Panther* films.

Gap: An unfilled space or interval, a break in continuity.

Gap financing: When equity, presales, and soft money are added up and don't reach the full budget required to make a film, the difference is called gap financing. Gap is usually provided by individual equity investors who, by investing the gap, take a lesser risk than investors who provided the initial equity. They are normally repaid first, and generally do not retain an ongoing interest in the film's profits. Sometimes called "bridge financing," or "mezzanine financing."

Gatekeeper: An attendant at a gate employed to control who goes through it, and therefore applied to anyone who must pass judgment on a story before it achieves publication or production. In story structure, a gatekeeper, like Cerberus at the entrance to Hades, guards secret knowledge, treasure, or a kingdom.

Genre: A "category" or "kind" of story, like dramatic romance, romantic comedy, action, action-adventure, epic, sci-fi, that contains story elements that the audience considers obligatory.

Gimme: A single unlikely thing the audience allows the storyteller to use in setting up his story, as in "what if a boy believed he was a bird." Aka "McGuffin."

Going wide: An expression that means the person who's selling your story is submitting it to many buyers at once, instead of using the selective approach.

Gothic: A type of story with dark and mysterious settings, or bizarre violence and/or characters.

Greenlight: Entertainment term for the moment all comes together in the making of a film or show, often provided by the financing entity.

Gross: The total revenues from an entertainment or publishing project, before any deductions for manufacturing or production, distribution, exhibition, promotion, taxes, etc.

Guardian: A supporting character that protects the protagonist from harm.

Hero: The lead character in a story, a.k.a. protagonist, whose courage and determination are tested by the obstacles he encounters.

High concept: A term used for stories that have the widest possible audiences, often further characterized by the brevity with which they can be pitched. *The Martian:* He was left behind. On Mars. *Red Sparrow:* Her uncle had her trained. To kill him.

Hollywood: "Hollywood" has long ago become the metaphorical word for referring to the entertainment business mostly centered in greater Los Angeles—ranging from Santa Monica to Burbank, from Beverly Hills to Valencia, but not really in Hollywood-proper. The actual Hollywood, where Hollywood Boulevard is, is where you find the tourist attraction Grauman's Chinese Theater as well as the Hollywood sign and the Dolby Theater where the Academy Awards presentation takes place.

Hook: The story element that compels the audience to keep reading or watching, ideally in the very opening of the story.

Hyphenate: An entertainment person who plays more than one role in the business, like a writer-director, manager-producer, or actor-producer.

Image: An artistic representation of the external form of a person or thing.

Imitation: Aristotle, in his *Poetics*, defined drama as the *imitation* of a powerful action in such a way that its importance is clear enough to move the audience.

In medias res: Latin for "in the middle of things," the place where a well-told story should start.

Inciting incident: The action or event, at the opening of a story, that establishes the dramatic trajectory of the remainder of the story.

Independent film: A feature film produced outside the major film studio system.

Independent producer: A producer who is not employed by a motion picture studio but makes movies independently.

Indie: Short for *independent*.

Intellectual property a.k.a. "I.P.": As distinguished from *real property* like a house, a piece of land, or a shoe, I.P. refers to a story or other form of entertainment created by the human brain and perceived to have value to the story marketplace.

Intensity rating: A graph (see pp. 48ff) we first presented in *Writing Treatments That Sell* that charts the rise and fall of action in a story on a scene-by-scene basis.

Internal story: A story that relies too much on the characters' thoughts and narrated feelings to the point that it becomes difficult to dramatize.

I.P.: Short for "intellectual property," the legal term describing any kind of story material created by an author and transmitted by legal contract to a buyer who intends to make a motion picture or television program based on it.

Lard Factor: Richard Lanham's term for verbal fat. "Your Lard Factor is 50%" means you use twice as many words as you need to tell your story effectively.

Legacy publisher: A traditional publishing company with a long history that still publishes books in the pre-internet pattern of doing business.

Legs: Entertainment industry term for a story's ability to merit more than one season of episodes.

Legitimate stage: Professional, high quality theater as opposed to vaudeville, burlesque, or comedy.

Life rights: The intellectual property rights to a person's biographical information, from birth to the present point; or for any part of the life that's agreed upon by the seller and purchaser of the rights.

Limited series: A series, like *Genius,* is a drama in as many episodes as needed to get the story told, as opposed to an ongoing series that runs from one season to another.

Line producer: This is the producer who physically produces the film by being present on the line as shooting is planned and carried out, and being conscious of, and responsible for, every line of the budget. A line producer is distinguished from a creative producer, who isn't responsible for the nuts and bolts of production, though both functions can be performed by the same person

Literary manager: A person who represents storytellers and also produces movies.

Live action: A term used to differentiate animation from dramatization of a story using actors.

Location: A venue used to film a scene or scenes.

Location scout: Before a film commences production, locations must be chosen for each scene in the story. The location scout is the specialist in each shooting jurisdiction who knows where to find the right kind of house, the right terrain, the right river or lake to fit the story. He or she is generally put to work late in the development process and before preproduction to analyze the script and suggest locations by photos send to the director by internet to help in the planning of the shoot.

Logline: A one-line pitch of your story, very much like the one-liners you would read in *TV Guide*. Also known as an "elevator pitch," or "one-liner."

Long-form television. A television term used to differentiate series programming like *Scandal* or *Breaking Bad* when they've been broadcast for at least one season.

Major studio motion picture: A movie produced and distributed by one of the "major studios"—Disney, Columbia, Fox, Paramount, Universal, Warner Brothers.

Make: The manufacturer or trade name of a particular commercial product.

Manuscript: Technically, the term refers to a book or other piece of intellectual property written by hand; but generically it's come to mean a written intellectual property, whether by hand or not.

Marketing array: Various forms of the pitch for your story: treatment, logline, one-paragraph, etc.

MBA: Minimum Basic Agreement, of the Writers Guild of America.

McGuffin: The contrivance around which a plot is hung.

Messenger: Instigators, from Hermes to the old woman who knocks on the Prince's door in Disney's *Beauty and the Beast*.

Metanoia: Aristotle's term for the watershed moment when the protagonist changes or reverses his course.

Mezzanine: The level of financing that is in neither first or last position in a film financing structure.

Middle: The most challenging section of a story that lies between the beginning (a.k.a. *hook*) and the end (a.k.a. *resolution*).

Mimesis: Aristotle's (Greek) word for *imitation*.

Mise en scène: The putting together of all the elements that comprise the physical set on which a story scene is to be shot.

Mission: The protagonist's objective set up in the beginning of a story, also known as his or her quest.

Monologue: An unrealistically long speech by a given character in a story.

Motif: A recurring element in a story, like rain on the window, a surly smile, demanding questions, or a stray dog that barks at the signs of danger.

Motion picture a.k.a. film a.k.a. movie. Technically, a series of images that when edited together give the appearance of motion.

Motivation: The reason or complex of reasons a character acts in a particular way.

Multiple submission: The offering of an intellectual property to more than one buyer at the same time.

Myth: A story so ancient no one can be sure who first told it. If there are, as some think, only a limited number of stories in human experience, their original form we call myth.

Mythic substructure: The archetypal structure from which a story draws for its overall arc, as in "The Labors of Hercules" or "Man against Dragon."

Narrative: The structure of a story, told by the narrator or fictional storyteller.

Negative cost: Entertainment accounting term used to describe the all-in cost to produce and shoot a motion picture or television program.

Negative pickup: Entertainment term used to describe a contractual promise from a studio or distributor to pay an agreed-upon amount upon delivery of the film to the purchaser of specified distribution rights.

Net: Financial term referring to what is left after all fees, expenses, and other costs are deducted. *Net* is the opposite of *gross*. The definition of net profits is one of the most hotly-contested issues in the story marketplace.

Novel: A more or less lengthy fictitious narrative telling a story through characters, dialogue, and action.

Novella: A shorter fictitious narrative, longer than a *short story* but not long enough to be called a *novel*.

Obligatory action or scenes: The actions or scenes in a story that *must be physically shown* for the story to make sense.

Obstacle: An impediment to the protagonist accomplishing his mission in the story. It can be a person, a mountain, a runaway train—all "obstacles" to the hero's progress.

On the nose: A derogatory term to describe dialogue (or events) that are so clearly expository that they interrupt the flow of the story and threaten its credibility.

One-liner: The pitch of a story in a few words, no longer than one line if possible: "Left behind. On Mars." A.k.a. logline.

Option: In the process of purchasing an intellectual property, an option is the first step allowing a certain period, in exchange for an *option payment,* for the purchaser to come up with the *purchase price.* That final moment is referred to as *exercising the option.*

Option price: The price paid to a holder of underlying rights (treatment, book, screenplay, etc.) to allow the buyer a specified amount of time to set up all the elements required for the movie to be made.

Option-purchase agreement: The standard agreement by which a buyer acquires control over an I.P. by optioning it for a certain price for a certain period of time, with a promise to purchase it by a certain date—or return all rights back to the creator.

Original screenplay: As opposed to an "adaptation," an original screenplay is not derived from an underlying intellectual property but is composed by the originator of the story directly into screenplay form.

Originality: The ability to think independently and creatively, ideally of a story not overly told before.

Overview: A bird's-eye pitch of a story.

Over the top: Generally critical term describing action or other dramatic element that is excessive in making its point and therefore not aesthetically pleasing.

Over the transom: Antiquated term for a literary property that makes its way to an acquisitions editor or acquisitions executive without an agent, manager, attorney, or other professional representation.

Packaging: The Hollywood practice of "attaching elements" to a story, such as director, screenwriter, or stars before submitting the project for financing. Packaging agents, like CAA, ICM, or WME receive a percentage of a film's production budget for packaging it;

which means that their clients who are part of the "package" aren't charged their usual ten percent agency fee.

Paragraph: A block of words in a written narrative, dealing with a single theme or character and marked by a new line or indentation. There is no set rule for how long or short a paragraph may be.

Participation: Someone's share of a motion picture's profits.

Pass: The word used in Hollywood instead of "rejection."

Pay or play: A contract, rarely offered to anyone but star actors or directors, that guarantees payment whether the film is produced or not.

Payoff: Refers to the moment of "reveal" when a foreshadowed element in a drama becomes fully apparent to the audience.

Period piece: Hollywood term for any program whose story is not contemporary, meaning any story whose setting is older than ten years or so. Period pieces include *Hostiles, Sherlock Holmes,* and *Rome.*

Personal point of view: Refers to the point of view from which a story is told, generally in the first person.

Pitch: An oral presentation of a story, intended to sell the listener on it immediately. A pitch can be oral or written.

Pitch line: The shortest pitch of a story a.k.a. logline.

Platform: A storyteller's social network of potential readers who might want to read his or her story.

Plot, or plotline: The main events of a story, presented by the writer as an interrelated set of events.

POD: Print on demand—the practice of printing books as they are purchased, as opposed to the traditional practice of printing books in advance on the hopes they will sell.

POV: Screenwriting shorthand for "point of view."

Point of View: The storyteller's relationship to his or her story, also related to the viewpoint from which the story is told.

Points: Entertainment accounting slang for "percentage points," usually of the backend profits of a produced project. Sometimes referred to as "Monkey points."

Polish: Screenwriting term for a relatively light revision of a screenplay.

Postproduction: The filmmaking phase that begins the last day of principal photography, and sometimes even earlier, in which the film is edited, sound and visual effects and music added, and all mixed with the images until the film is finalized.

Preempt, a.k.a. preemptive bid: A bid whose intention is to take the story off the market immediately and is therefore accompanied by a short deadline for response. For example, a studio will make an offer and give the seller's representative a few hours to respond to it before removing the offer from the table.

Premise: Same as **concept,** the one sentence that encapsulates an entire story and permeates its every scene: "Overwhelming ambition leads to self-destruction" (see Lajos Egri, *The Art of Dramatic Writing*). The answer to the question, "What is this story about?"

Prep: Short for "preproduction," the period before the actual filming of a movie begins, during which all facets of the production are brought to readiness for the filming.

Preproduction: Production of an entertainment project is divided into preproduction when a production office is set up, accounting established, locations surveyed and chosen, cast finalized, script finalized, etc.; production proper, a.k.a. "principal photography," when the camera rolls and the scenes of the drama are recorded on film or tape or digitally; and "postproduction" when the film is edited, and music, sounds effects, color correction, and visual effects are perfected. The period before production is referred to as "development," and after production is "distribution."

Prequel: A story that comes before another story, like *The Hobbit* coming before *The Lord of the Rings.*

Press: Newspapers, magazines, and blogs viewed collectively.

Presales: Term for licensing a film to a particular foreign or domestic territory before the film is actually produced, often used to contribute to the overall funding required to shoot the film. Presales are disadvantageous compared to sales made when the film is finished and offered to buyers.

Pre-sold audience: A film project that can claim it's already a household name, like the many Marvel comics or *Lord of the Rings.*

Principal photography: The day when the film begins shooting; when the cameras first roll.

Producer: Responsible for the entire production, promotion, and distribution of a film; and often originating it as well. "The producer's the one who turns on the lights in the morning and turns them off at the end of the day."

Product placement: In a film or show for television or theater, featuring a commercial object on screen or stage in exchange for a fee.

Production: The physical process by which a screenplay or teleplay is turned into a motion picture or television program. Although "production" can refer to the entire process, the word can also be used to differentiate the first part of the process—**preproduction,** which includes location scouting, extra casting, production design, setting up accounting, etc.--from beginning of principal photography to its end (see **wrap**)—from the activities that occur during postproduction, including editing, insertion of special visual effects and music, color correction, etc.

Production timeline: A calendar of the steps required in the making of a film, listing the projected commencement of each.

Prologue: A separate, introductory, section of a story.

Prop: Short for "property," any object that goes before the camera during principal photography, from pictures on the wall to the furniture in a room.

Property: An object of value, whether physical (like a house) or intellectual (like a book or a patent) that belongs to its owner or proprietor.

Protagonist: The "first actor" in a drama, often called the hero. He is the prime cause of the action that unfolds, and the story is *about him*.

Psychology of the audience: British critic Kenneth Burke's term for the interaction between the audience of a drama and the story itself, which he considered more important for the storyteller to master than the psychology of his characters or even his or her own psychology.

Public domain: Refers to intellectual rights that are not under copyright, usually because they were written before the modern copyright era. It's called public domain because such property belongs to the public and anyone can use it without seeking permission or purchasing rights.

Purchase price: The price paid to a creator or holder of underlying rights, usually upon the first day of principal photography, to transfer all rights from the creator/holder to the buyer, thereby protecting the buyer's investment in the film.

Query or **Query Letter:** The industry term for an inquiry, most often by email, asking the person you've emailed if they are interested in your story.

Quote: As used in Hollywood, this refers to the highest amount a writer, actor, or director has been paid previously, usually on his or her last project, as in "Her quote is $150,000." The artist's objective is to get more than your previous quote on each new deal.

Release form: A legal form that protects a buyer (studio, production company, agency, etc.) from your potential claim that they have stolen your intellectual property. In almost all cases, I recommend you sign the release without question, though if you can afford to do so, it never hurts to show the form to an attorney.

Reluctant hero: A protagonist who has no wish to undertake his mission in the story and has to be dragged into it, like Frodo in *The Lord of the Rings*.

Residuals: Further payments received by artists when their films are rerun or sold to new markets.

Resolution: The final part of a story, when all the dramatic elements set in motion at the start are brought to conclusion.

Reveal: The moment in a story when a secret or hidden element is made clear to the audience, as when the culprit is identified in a mystery.

Reversal: An action taken by a character in a story that moves in the opposite of his previous actions or of the audience's expectations.

Reversion: The legal name for the return of intellectual property rights to their creator.

Rhythmic development: The rise and fall of dramatic action in a manner that keeps the audience fully engaged from beginning to end of a screenplay, especially in act two. Often referred to as "rising and falling action."

Romance: A story in which two lovers find each other and experience together a series of obstacles to their love until they either come together more or less happily or part sadly, as in *Witness*, or tragically, as in *Romeo and Juliet*.

Rushes: See **dailies**.

Sales agent: A representative who takes a film to the market, both foreign and domestic.

Scale: "Scale," most often in the context of the Screen Actors Guild (SAG), refers to a cast payment schedule tied to the overall budget of an entertainment project.

Scenario: A pattern in which events unfold; a written outline for a story.

Scene: The basic unit of drama in which a new conflict is faced by a character.

Screenplay: Hollywood term for the written document upon which a film is based, which serves as a kind of blueprint for dramatizing the story. A typical Hollywood screenplay ranges between 95-115 pages, though there are glaring exceptions especially on the long side.

Script doctor: An editor who points out, or fixes, the weaknesses in a script and assists the screenwriter in making it work on all fronts for the screen.

Sell sheet: A pitch of a story, on one page.

Sequel: A story that starts where a previous story ends, just as a prequel ends where another story begins.

Set: The decorated location in which a particular location is shot by the camera.

Setting: Term used for the place, in all its particulars, where a drama is set—often so important it becomes a major element of the story, as in *The Martian, The Thing, Passengers,* and *Titanic.*

Set-up: The opening of a novel or film, establishing the protagonist and his situation in life as well as key dramatic elements he will deal with. Also: Arranging for the financing of a motion picture; preparing a scene to be shot.

Shoot: Movies are said to be "shot" by the camera, with the director being the shooter, from old times when cameras were likened to guns. The word is both a verb, as in "let's shoot this picture this year," or a noun, as "Who do I have to sleep with to get off this shoot?"

Shooting script: The version of a movie or television script which the director uses as a guide to shooting the film.

Shop: The process of submitting your story to production companies, studios, financers, and broadcasters is called "shopping it," and an agreement to allow someone to do so is a "shopping agreement."

Short story: A dramatic story that is not long enough to be called a novel, ranging from a Richard Brautigan two-line short story to Leo Tolstoy "The Death of Ivan Ilych" (which some people call a novella). Great short story writers include Nathaniel Hawthorne ("Young Goodman Brown"), Franz Kafka "The Judgment," and Doris Lessing's "To Room 19."

Showrunner: The experienced person who guides the overall shape of a television series or limited series, usually a writer who has succeeded in a previous series.

Soft money: All the money used to produce a film that isn't equity—that is, hard cash—is called soft money. Soft money includes tax rebates, state or national incentives, loans, gifts, etc.

Spec: A shorthand for "speculation," usually referring to work done without compensation by a third party but on the hopes that it will lead to compensation, as in "writing on spec" a "spec script."

Spine: The main action line of a story.

Stakes: What's at risk in a story. A story with low stakes will have low reader interest.

Star: A charismatic and box-office-successful actor whose mere involvement in a film gets it financed and draws audiences to the box office.

Start date: The day on which everyone involved in the actual filming of the story is available to begin that crucial work. Start date usually refers to the commencement of preproduction.

Story editor: The title given to industry readers, who read stories for their executive, agent, manager, producer, and director bosses and report the story's potential and its flaws.

Structure: The arrangement of parts to form a whole.

Studio: A set of buildings designed for filmmaking, as well as the generic term for a company that own and operates such buildings.

Summary: Telling the story for the sake of clarity, as opposed to dramatizing the story.

Suspension of disbelief: The audience's or reader's willingness to suspend their critical faculties and accept something hard to believe, sacrificing realism for the sake of enjoying a story. The process by which the audience allows itself to believe a story is called "suspending their disbelief."

Sympathetic: The word comes originally from ancient Greek, where it means "to suffer along with" someone. Can we relate to him or her? If we can, he or she is a "sympathetic" character in our story.

Synopsis: A matter of fact summary of a story, just laying out its elements as the occur, often created by a story editor to give his or her boss an overview of the story so that he can fake his way through a meeting with the writer.

Syntax: Grammatical, logical, and expository rules that govern formal prose. Drama is known for shattering syntax with surprise, power, and unexpected turns.

Taking it out to the town: An expression that means the person who's selling your story is now ready to send it to buyers or creative allies.

Target audience: A target audience is a demographic of readers based on variables such as age, race, sex, interest, location, socioeconomic status, education, etc.

Target cast: A producer's wish-list of the cast desired for a proposed film, usually based on the relative availability of the cast listed. This is to be distinguished from the actual cast on hand upon commencement of principal photography.

Tax incentives: Some states or countries offer various incentives to induce filmmakers to bring their productions to their jurisdiction. This can range from sales tax abatement to tax-deductible allowances for their citizens who invest in these productions.

Tax rebates: Some states and countries offer filmmakers a percentage rebate for all monies the filmmaker spends in their jurisdiction, usually in the form of direct payment following a state- or country-certified audit.

Tax rebate incentive: Any program or incentive that reduces the amount of tax owed by an individual or business entity to the government issuing the incentive to promote commerce.

Teleplay: While a screenplay adapts a story for production as a motion picture, a teleplay adapts a story for television.

Theme: The "moral" or "lesson" the audience is left with after reading or seeing a story.

Through line: The "spine" of a story, the structural continuity that connects a story's ending with its beginning. The through line of a mystery begins with a murder and ends with the discovery of who the murderer is.

Ticking clock: A structural story device that gives the protagonist a limited amount of time to achieve his goal, as with any story where a bomb threatens to explode or a diver will run out of air if she doesn't surface soon enough.

Tone of voice: A particular quality of a storytelling voice that heightens the impact of the story's events; the attitude behind the storyteller's point of view: sarcastic, dead serious, cosmic, ironic, comic, etc.

Top sheet: A one-two-page summary of the 100+ pages detailed budget that shows the bottom line of every major line item from

Development to Deliverables, giving producers and financiers an overview of the total cost of producing a film. (See Appendix B for an example.)

Trackers: Independent contractors who hunt down those who control the rights to a given story, and report the information to their bosses (studios, production companies, directors, etc.).

Traditional publisher: Alternate name for "legacy publisher," a company that pays an advance to the author to publish his or her book and controls all their publishing rights in the pre-internet way of doing business.

Tragedy: A story with an unhappy ending and theme, in which a protagonist is defeated by the obstacles to his or her mission that are created by a flaw in his character, as when King Lear is brought down by the very daughters he plans to bequeath his kingdom to.

Treatment: A treatment is a relatively brief, loosely narrative, written pitch of a story intended for production as a film for theatrical exhibition or television broadcast. Written in user-friendly, dramatic but straightforward and highly visual prose in the present tense, the treatment highlights in broad strokes your story's hook, primary characters, acts and action line, setting, point of view, and most dramatic scenes and turning points.

Tunneling: The art of providing backstory to your story by inserting the backstory in dramatic spots where it's needed, without slowing the story down unnecessarily.

Turning point: See **Metanoia.**

Twist: A sudden turn of direction in a story's plot that surprises the protagonist and the audience.

Ulmer Scale: A survey that ranks on a scale of 1 to 100 the influence of more than 1,400 actors worldwide to generate movie financing. Created in 1998 by entertainment journalist James Ulmer, the survey canvases sources that range from producers, entertainment agents and studio executives to international distributors, foreign sales agents and investment bankers. Taken into account are an actor's box office numbers, versatility, professionalism and willingness to promote films.

Underlying Rights; Underlying Property; Underlying Material: Legal terminology for the story you created in every format in which it exists (book, pitch, and/or treatment), which is intellectual property owned by you until you sell it or make your own film based on it.

Vanity press: Outdated term referring to what today is known as direct publishing, where a business presents itself as a traditional publisher but charges the writer exorbitant fees to publish and store his or her book.

Watcher: A person who observes something regularly or attentively.

Worlds in collision: The kind of story in which characters from different worlds are thrown into conflict with each other, as in *Planet of the Apes* or *The Russians Are Coming, The Russians Are Coming.*

Young Adult: Readers aged 14 to 21.

SOURCES & RESOURCES

Advice on the Writer's Career:

Atchity, Kenneth. *A Writer's Time: A Guide to the Creative Process, from Vision through Revision.*

Atchity, Kenneth and Chi-Li Wong. *Writing Treatments That Sell: How to Create and Market Your Story Ideas to the Motion Picture and TV Industry.*

Atchity, Kenneth with Andrea McKeown, Julie Mooney, and Margaret O'Connor. *How to Publish Your Novel.*

Atchity, Kenneth. *Sell Your Story to Hollywood: Writer's Pocket Guide to the Business of Show Business.*

Bradbury, Ray. *Zen in the Art of Writing.*

Brandeis, Dorothea. *Becoming a Writer.*

Canfield, Jack, Mark Victor Hansen, and Bud Gardner. *Chicken Soup for the Author's Soul: Stories to Open the Heart and Rekindle the Spirit of Writers.*

Densham, Pen and Jay Roach. *Riding the Alligator: Strategies for a Career in Screenplay Writing (and not getting eaten).*

Egri, Lajos. *The Art of Dramatic Writing.*

Evanovich, Janet and Ina Yalof. *How I Write: Secrets of a Serial Fiction Writer.*

Gardner, John. *On Moral Fiction.*

Gerth, Sandra. *Point of View: How to Use the Different Point of View Types, avoid head-hopping, and Choose the Best Point of View for Your Book.*

Kennedy, Mary. *Point of View.*

King, Stephen. *On Writing*

Koontz, Dean R. *How to Write Best Selling Fiction.*

McKee, Robert. *Story: Substance, Style and the Principles of Screenwriting.*

Noble, June and Thomas. *Steal This Plot.*

Rubie, Peter. *The Elements of Storytelling: How to Write Compelling Fiction.*

See, Carolyn. *Making a Literary Life: Advice for Writers and Other Dreamers.*

Seger, Linda. *Making a Good Script Great.*

Stein, Sol. *Stein on Writing: A Master Editor of Some of the Most Successful Writers of Our Century Shares His Craft Techniques and Strategies.*

Turco, Lewis. *The Book of Dialogue: How to Write Effective Conversation in Fiction, Screenplays, Drama, and Poetry.*

Whitney, Phyllis A. *Writing Juvenile Stories and Novels: How to Write and Sell Fiction for Young People.*

Reference Books:

Abbe, Elfriede Martha. *The Writer's Handbook.*

The Chicago Manual of Style.

Fowler's Modern Usage.

Judd, Karen. *Copyediting: A Practical Guide.*

Lanham, Richard A. *Revising Prose.*

Princeton Language Institute. *Roget's 21ˢᵗ Century Thesaurus in Dictionary Form.*

Ross-Larson, Bruce. *Edit Yourself: A Manual for Everyone Who Works with Words.*

Stilman, Anne. *Grammatically Correct: The Essential Guide to Spelling, Style, Usage, Grammar, and Punctuation.*

Strunk, William H. and E. B. White. *The Elements of Style.*

Marketing References:

Brewer, Robert Lee. *Writer's Market.*

Brewer, Robert Lee. *Poet's Market.*

Freese, Cris. *Songwriter's Market: Where & How to Market Your Songs.*

Hollywood Reporter. *The Hollywood Creative Directory.*

Hollywood Creative Directory Staff. *Hollywood Representation Directory*.

Herman, Jeff. *Jeff Herman's Guide to Book Publishers, Editors and Literary Agents: Who They Are, What They Want, and How to Win Them Over*.

Literary Marketplace

Perez, Dinah, and Jesse Douma. *Hollywood Screenwriting Directory Fall/Winter: A Specialized Resource for Discovering Where & How to Sell Your Screenplay*.

Randall, Rachel. *Novel & Short Story Writer's Market*.

Sambuchino, Chuck. *Children's Writer's and Illustrator's Market*.

Sambuchino, Chuck. *Guide to Literary Agents*.

TELL
YOUR
STORY
to the
WORLD
& SELL IT FOR
# MILLIONS

Made in the USA
Columbia, SC
29 October 2020